Helen Hunt Jackson

Verses

Helen Hunt Jackson

Verses

ISBN/EAN: 9783743328396

Manufactured in Europe, USA, Canada, Australia, Japa

Cover: Foto ©Thomas Meinert / pixelio.de

Manufactured and distributed by brebook publishing software (www.brebook.com)

Helen Hunt Jackson

Verses

DEDICATION.

WHEN children in the summer weather play,
Flitting like birds through sun and wind and rain,
From road to field, from field to road again,
Pathetic reckoning of each mile they stray
They leave in flowers forgotten by the way;
Forgotten, dying, but not all in vain,
Since, finding them, with tender smiles, half pain,
Half joy, we sigh, "Some child passed here to-day."
Dear one, — whose name I name not lest some tongue
Pronounce it roughly, — like a little child
Tired out at noon, I left my flowers among
The wayside things. I know how thou hast smiled,
And that the thought of them will always be
One more sweet secret thing 'twixt thee and me.

CONTENTS.

	Page
A Christmas Symphony	9
Spinning	14
My Legacy	16
Love's Largess	18
Found Frozen	20
My Days	21
The Zone of Calms	21
Message	22
My Lighthouses	23
In Time of Famine	25
The Prince is dead	26
Poppies on the Wheat	27
A Funeral March	28
Joy	33
Two Truths	34
Gondolieds	35
"Spoken"	37
The Way to Sing	39
The True Ballad of the King's Singer	41
Œnone	45
The Loneliness of Sorrow	47
A Sunrise	48
A Ballad of the Gold Country	49
Exile	55
My Ship	55
At Last	56
Memoir of a Queen	58
Our Angels	59
Mazzini	61
"When the Tide comes in"	61

CONTENTS.

	Page
THE SINGER'S HILLS	63
COVERT	68
WAITING	69
RENUNCIATION	70
BURNT SHIPS	71
RESURGAM	72
THE VILLAGE LIGHTS	79
TRANSPLANTED	80
BEST	82
MORNING-GLORY	83
OCTOBER	84
MY BEES	85
THE ABBOT PAPHNUTIUS	86
NOON	90
IN THE PASS	92
AMREETA WINE	94
SOLITUDE	96
NOT AS I WILL	97
LAND	99
OPPORTUNITY	100
WHEN THE BABY DIED	100
"OLD LAMPS FOR NEW"	102
FEAST	103
TWO SUNDAYS	105
SHOWBREAD	106
TIDES	107
TRIBUTE	107
"ALMS AT THE BEAUTIFUL GATE"	108
CORONATION	109
MY NEW FRIEND	111
ASTERS AND GOLDEN ROD	112
TWO LOVES	113
THE GOOD SHEPHERD	117
LOVE'S FULFILLING	118
WOOED	119
WON	120
ARIADNE'S FAREWELL	121
THOUGHT	121
MORDECAI	122
LOCUSTS AND WILD HONEY	123

CONTENTS.

A Mother's Farewell to a Voyager	124
"Dropped Dead"	125
Presence	126
Polar Days	127
Truth	127
Her Eyes	128
The Wall-Flower of the Ruins of Rome	129
Shadows of Birds	130
Glimpses	131
To A. C. L. B.	132
Snow-Drops in Italy	132
Distance	133
When the Kings come	134
Coming across	134
The Teacher	135
Decoration Day	136
A 13th-Century Parable	138
Form	141
My Hickory Fire	142
Revenues	144
A Burial Service	146
A Parable	147
Friends	148
The Royal Beggar	149
March	149
April	150
May	151
The Simple King	152
The Singer's Friends	155
Doubt	157
Forgiven	158
This Summer	158
Tryst	160
The Magic Armory	161
Lifted over	162
My House not made with Hands	163
My Strawberry	166
Triumph	167
Return to the Hills	168
"Down to Sleep"	170

CONTENTS.

	Page
Fallow	171
Love's Rich and Poor	173
Light on the Mountain-tops	174
Christmas Night in St. Peter's	175
Welcome	177
The Two Comrades	178
Demeter	181
Expectancy	182
Belated	182
To an Unknown Lady	185
A Wild Rose in September	187
Arctic Quest	188
The Sign of the Daisy	189
Vintage	190
Last Words	191

A CHRISTMAS SYMPHONY.

I.

 CHRISTMAS stars! your pregnant silentness,
Mute syllabled in rhythmic light,
Leads on to-night,
And beckons, as three thousand years ago
It beckoning led. We, simple shepherds, know
    Little we can confess,
Beyond that we are poor, and creep
And wander with our sheep,
    Who love and follow us. We hear,
If we attend, a singing in the sky;
    But feel no fear,
Knowing that God is always nigh,
And none pass by,
Except His Sons, who cannot bring
Tidings of evil, since they sing.
Wise men with gifts are hurrying,

In haste to seek the meaning of the Star,
In search of worship which is new and far.
    We are but humble, so we keep
        On through the night, contented with our
    sheep,
And with the stars. Between us and the east,
  No wall, no tree, no cloud, lifts bar.
We know the sunrise. Not one least
    Of all its tokens can escape
  Our eyes that watch. But all days are
As nights, and nights as days,
In our still ways.
    We have no dread of any shape
      Which darkness can assume or fill;
  We are not weary; we can wait;
  God's hours are never late.
The wise men say they will return,
Revealing unto us the things they learn.
    Mayhap! Meantime the Star stands still;
And, having that, we have the Sign.
If we mistake, God is divine!

II.

Oh, not alone because His name is Christ,
    Oh, not alone because Judea waits
  This man-child for her King, the Star stands still.
    Its glory reinstates,
  Beyond humiliation's utmost ill,
    On peerless throne, which she alone can fill,
Each earthly woman. Motherhood is priced

Of God, at price no man may dare
To lessen, or misunderstand.
The motherhood which came
To virgin sets in vestal flame,
Fed by each new-born infant's hand,
With Heaven's air,
With Heaven's food,
The crown of purest purity revealed,
Virginity eternal signed and sealed
Upon all motherhood!

III.

Oh, not alone because His name is Christ,
Oh, not alone because Judea waits
This man-child for her King, the Star stands still.
The Babe has mates.
Childhood shall be forever on the earth;
And no man who has hurt or lightly priced
So much as one sweet hair
On one sweet infant's head,
But shall be cursed! Henceforth all things fulfil
Protection to each sacred birth.
No spot shall dare
Refuse a shelter. Beasts shall tread
More lightly; and distress,
And poverty, and loneliness,
Yea, and all darkness, shall devise
To shield each place wherein an infant lies.
And wisdom shall come seeking it with gift,
And worship it with myrrh and frankincense;

And kings shall tremble if it lift
    Its hand against a throne.
    But mighty in its own
Great feebleness, and safe in God's defence,
    No harm can touch it, and no death can kill,
    Without its Father's will!

IV.

Oh, not alone because His name is Christ,
    Oh, not alone because Judea waits
    This man-child for her King, the Star stands still.
    The universe must utter, and fulfil
        The mighty voice which states,
    The mighty destiny which holds,
        Its key-note and its ultimate design.
    Waste places and the deserts must perceive
That they are priced,
        No less than gardens in the Heart Divine.
Sorrow her sorrowing must leave,
    And learn one sign
        With joy. And Loss and Gain
        Must be no more.
And all things which have gone before,
        And all things which remain,
        And all of Life, and all of Death be slain
        In mighty birth, whose name
Is called Redemption ! Praise !
    Praise to God ! 'The same
To-day and yesterday, and in all days
    Forever ! Praise !

V.

Oh, Christmas stars! Your pregnant silentness,
    Mute syllabled in rhythmic light,
    Fills all the night.
No doubt, on all your golden shores,
    Full music rings
    Of Happiness
    As sweet as ours.
Midway in that great tideless stream which pours,
    And builds its shining road through trackless space,
From you to us, and us to you, must be
    Some mystic place,
Where all our voices meet, and melt
Into this solemn silence which is felt,
    And sense of sound mysterious brings
Where sound is not. This is God's secret. He
    Sits centred in his myriads of skies,
    Where seas of sound and seas of silence rise,
And break together in one note and key,
    Divinely limitless in harmony!

SPINNING.

LIKE a blind spinner in the sun,
    I tread my days;
I know that all the threads will run
    Appointed ways;
I know each day will bring its task,
And, being blind, no more I ask.

I do not know the use or name
    Of that I spin;
I only know that some one came,
    And laid within
My hand the thread, and said, "Since you
Are blind, but one thing you can do."

Sometimes the threads so rough and fast
    And tangled fly,
I know wild storms are sweeping past,
    And fear that I
Shall fall; but dare not try to find
A safer place, since I am blind.

I know not why, but I am sure
    That tint and place,
In some great fabric to endure
    Past time and race
My threads will have; so from the first,
Though blind, I never felt accurst.

I think, perhaps, this trust has sprung
    From one short word
Said over me when I was young,—
    So young, I heard
It, knowing not that God's name signed
My brow, and sealed me his, though blind.

But whether this be seal or sign
    Within, without,
It matters not. The bond divine
    I never doubt.
I know he set me here, and still,
And glad, and blind, I wait His will;

But listen, listen, day by day,
    To hear their tread
Who bear the finished web away,
    And cut the thread,
And bring God's message in the sun,
"Thou poor blind spinner, work is done."

MY LEGACY.

THEY told me I was heir, I turned in haste,
    And ran to seek my treasure,
And wondered as I ran how it was placed,—
    If I should find a measure
Of gold, or if the titles of fair lands
And houses would be laid within my hands.

I journeyed many roads ; I knocked at gates ;
    I spoke to each wayfarer
I met, and said, "A heritage awaits
    Me. Art not thou the bearer
Of news ? Some message sent to me whereby
I learn which way my new possessions lie ? "

Some asked me in ; naught lay beyond their door ;
    Some smiled and would not tarry,
But said that men were just behind who bore
    More gold than I could carry ;
And so the morn, the noon, the day were spent,
While empty-handed up and down I went.

At last one cried, whose face I could not see,
    As through the mists he hasted ;
"Poor child, what evil ones have hindered thee,
    Till this whole day is wasted ?
Hath no man told thee that thou art joint heir
With one named Christ, who waits the goods to
    share ? "

MY LEGACY.

The one named Christ I sought for many days,
   In many places vainly;
I heard men name his name in many ways;
   I saw his temples plainly;
But they who named him most gave me no sign
To find him by, or prove the heirship mine.

And when at last I stood before his face,
   I knew him by no token
Save subtle air of joy which filled the place;
   Our greeting was not spoken;
In solemn silence I received my share,
Kneeling before my brother and "joint heir."

My share! No deed of house or spreading lands,
   As I had dreamed; no measure
Heaped up with gold; my elder brother's hands
   Had never held such treasure.
Foxes have holes, and birds in nests are fed:
My brother had not where to lay his head.

My share! The right like him to know all pain
   Which hearts are made for knowing;
The right to find in loss the surest gain;
   To reap my joy from sowing
In bitter tears; the right with him to keep
A watch by day and night with all who weep.

My share! To-day men call it grief and death;
   I see the joy and life to-morrow;

I thank our Father with my every breath,
    For this sweet legacy of sorrow;
And through my tears I call to each, "Joint heir
With Christ, make haste to ask him for thy share."

LOVE'S LARGESS.

AT my heart's door
    Love standeth, like a king beside
    His royal treasury, whose wide
    Gates open swing, and cannot hide
        Their priceless store.

        His touch and hold
Its common things to jewels turned;
In his sweet fires the dross he burned
Away; and thus he won and earned
        And made its gold.

        So rich I find
Myself in service of this king,
The goods we spare, in alms I fling;
And breathless days too few hours bring
        Me to be kind,

        To souls whose pain
My heart can scarcely dare to greet
With pity, while my own complete

And blessed joy their loss must mete
    By my great gain.

    Diviner air
Of beauty, and a grace more free,
More soft and solemn depths I see
In every woman's face, since he
    Has called me fair.

    More true and sure
Each man's heart seems, more firm for right;
Each man I hold more strong in fight,
Since he stands ever in my sight,
    So brave, so pure.

    More of sun's fire
Than days can use, and more than nights
Can name, of stars with rhythmic lights,
And sweetest singing flocks, whose flights
    Can never tire, —

    More bloom than eyes
Can reach, or hands to grasp may dare, —
More music in the constant air,
Than each round wave can hold and bear,
    Before it dies, —

    And more of life
For living, than all death can kill,
More good than evil's utmost will
Can thwart, and peace to more than still
    The fiercest strife, —

All these I find
In service of this gracious king;
From goods we spare, such alms I fling;
And pray swift days more hours to bring,
More bonds to bind.

O happiness!
To utter thee, in vain our eyes
Seek tears; and vainly all speech tries;
This thing alone our king denies
In Love's largess.

FOUND FROZEN.

SHE died, as many travellers have died,
O'ertaken on an Alpine road by night;
Numbed and bewildered by the falling snow,
Striving, in spite of failing pulse, and limbs
Which faltered and grew feeble at each step,
To toil up the icy steep, and bear
Patient and faithful to the last, the load
Which, in the sunny morn, seemed light!
And yet
'T was in the place she called her home, she died;
And they who loved her with the all of love
Their wintry natures had to give, stood by
And wept some tears, and wrote above her grave
Some common record which they thought was true;
But I, who loved her last and best, — *I* knew.

MY DAYS

VEILED priestess, in a holy place,
Day pauseth on her threshold, beckoning;
As infants to the mother's bosom spring
At sound of mother's voice, although her face
Be hid, I leap with sudden joy. No trace
Of fear I feel; I take her hand and fling
Her arm around my neck, and walk and cling
Close to her side. She chooses road and pace;
I feast along the way on her shewbread;
I help an hour or two on her great task;
Beyond this honoring, no wage I ask.
Then, ere I know, sweet night slips in her stead,
And, while by sunset fires I rest and bask,
Warm to her faithful breast she folds my head.

THE ZONE OF CALMS.*

S yearning currents from the trackless snows,
And silent Polar seas, unceasing sweep
To South, to North, and linger not where leap
Red fires from glistening cones, — nor where the rose
Has triumph on the snow-fed Paramos,

---

* The Zone of Calms is the space comprised between the second degree north latitude and the second degree south.

In upper air, — nor yet where lifts the deep
Its silver Atolls on whose bosoms sleep
The purple sponges ; and, as in repose
Meeting at last, they sink upon the breast
Of that sweet tropic sea, whose spicy balms
And central heat have drawn them to its arms, —
So soul seeks soul, unsatisfied, represt,
Till in Love's tropic met, they sink to rest,
At peace forever, in the "Zone of Calms."

MESSAGE.

FOR one to bear my message, I looked out
    In haste, at noon. The bee and swallow passed
    Bound south. My message was to South.
    I cast
It trusting as a mariner. No doubt,
Sweet bee, blithe swallow, in my heart about
Your fellowship. The stealthy night came fast.
"O chilly night," I said, "no friend thou hast
For me, and morn is far," when lo ! a shout
Of joy, and riding up as one rides late,
My friend fell on my neck just in the gate.
"You got my message then ? "
                      "No message, sweet,
Save my own eyes' desire your eyes to meet."

"You saw no swallow and no bee before
You came?"
    "I do remember past my door
There brushed a bird and bee. O, dearer presage
Than I had dreamed! You sent by them a message?"

MY LIGHTHOUSES.

AT westward window of a palace gray,
 Which its own secret still so safely keeps
 That no man now its builder's name can say,
I lie and idly sun myself to-day,
Dreaming awake far more than one who sleeps,
Serenely glad, although my gladness weeps.

I look across the harbor's misty blue,
And find and lose that magic shifting line
Where sky one shade less blue meets sea, and through
The air I catch one flush as if it knew
Some secret of that meeting, which no sign
Can show to eyes so far and dim as mine.

More ships than I can count build mast by mast
Gay lattice-work with waving green and red
Across my window-panes. The voyage past,

They crowd to anchorage so glad, so fast,
Gliding like ghosts, with noiseless breath and tread,
Mooring like ghosts, with noiseless iron and lead.

" O ships and patient men who fare by sea,"
I stretch my hands and vainly questioning cry,
" Sailed ye from west? How many nights could ye
Tell by the lights just where my dear and free
And lovely land lay sleeping? Passed ye by
Some danger safe, because her fires were nigh?"

Ah me! my selfish yearning thoughts forget
How darkness but a hand's-breadth from the coast
With danger in an evil league is set!
Ah! helpless ships and men more helpless yet,
Who trust the land-lights' short and empty boast;
The lights ye bear aloft and prayers avail ye most.

But I — ah, patient men who fare by sea,
Ye would but smile to hear this empty speech, —
I have such beacon-lights to burn for me,
In that dear west so lovely, new, and free,
That evil league by day, by night, can teach
No spell whose harm my little bark can reach.

No towers of stone uphold those beacon-lights;
No distance hides them, and no storm can shake;
In valleys they light up the darkest nights,
They outshine sunny days on sunny heights;
They blaze from every house where sleep or wake
My own who love me for my own poor sake.

Each thought they think of me lights road of flame
Across the seas ; no travel on it tires
My heart. I go if they but speak my name ;
From Heaven I should come and go the same,
And find this glow forestalling my desires.
My darlings, do you hear me? Trim the fires !

    GENOA, November 30.

IN TIME OF FAMINE.

"HE has no heart," they said, and turned away,
    Then, stung so that I wished my words might be
Two-edged swords, I answered low : —

                              "Have ye
Not read how once when famine held fierce sway
In Lydia, and men died day by day
Of hunger, there were found brave souls whose glee
Scarce hid their pangs, who said, ' Now we
Can eat but once in two days ; we will play
Such games on those days when we eat no food
That we forget our pain.'

                      "Thus they withstood
Long years of famine ; and to them we owe
The trumpets, pipes, and balls which mirth finds good

To-day, and little dreams that of such woe
They first were born.
                "That woman's life I know
Has been all famine.   Mock now if ye dare,
To hear her brave sad laughter in the air."

THE PRINCE IS DEAD.

A ROOM in the palace is shut.   The king
And the queen are sitting in black.
All day weeping servants will run and
    bring,
But the heart of the queen will lack
All things; and the eyes of the king will swim
With tears which must not be shed,
But will make all the air float dark and dim,
As he looks at each gold and silver toy,
And thinks how it gladdened the royal boy,
And dumbly writhes while the courtiers read
How all the nations his sorrow heed.
            The Prince is dead.

The hut has a door, but the hinge is weak,
And to-day the wind blows it back;
There are two sitting there who do not speak;
They have begged a few rags of black.
They are hard at work, though their eyes are wet
With tears which must not be shed;

They dare not look where the cradle is set;
They hate the sunbeam which plays on the floor,
But will make the baby laugh out no more;
They feel as if they were turning to stone,
They wish the neighbors would leave them alone.
                        The Prince is dead.

POPPIES ON THE WHEAT.

LONG Ancona's hills the shimmering heat,
    A tropic tide of air with ebb and flow
    Bathes all the fields of wheat until they glow
Like flashing seas of green, which toss and beat
Around the vines. The poppies lithe and fleet
Seem running, fiery torchmen, to and fro
To mark the shore.   The farmer does not know
That they are there. He walks with heavy feet,
Counting the bread and wine by autumn's gain,
But I, — I smile to think that days remain
Perhaps to me in which, though bread be sweet
No more, and red wine warm my blood in vain,
I shall be glad remembering how the fleet,
Lithe poppies ran like torchmen with the wheat.

A FUNERAL MARCH.

I.

YES, all is ready now; the door and gate
  Have opened this last time for him, more
    wide
  Than is their wont; no longer side by side
 With us, he passes out; we follow, meek,
And weeping at his pomp, which is not pride,
  And which he did not seek.
We cannot speak,
Because we loved him so; we hesitate,
And cling and linger and in vain belate
Their feet who bear him.
    Slow, slow, slow,
With every fibre holding back, we go;
  And cruel hands, while we are near,
  And weep afresh to hear,
Have shut the door and shut the gate.

II.

  The air is full of shapes
    We do not see, but feel;
  Ghosts which no death escapes.
    No sepulchre can seal;
Ghosts of forgotten things of joy and grief;
  And ghosts of things which never were,
  But promised him to be: they may defer
Their pledges now; his unbelief

Is justified.   Oh, why did they abide
This time, these restless ghosts, which glide,
   Accompanying him?   Can they go in
Unquestioned, and confront him in the grave,
      And answers win
From dead lips which the live lips never gave?
Will they return across the churchyard gate
With us, weeping with us, "Too late! too late!"
   Or are they dead, as he is dead?
   And when the burial rites are said,
Will they lie down, the resurrection to await?

III.

With dumb, pathetic look the poor beasts go
At unaccustomed pace to suit our woe;
   Uncomprehending equally
Or what a grief or what a joy may be.
House after house where life makes glad
We bear him past, who all of life has had.
And men's and women's wistful eyes
Look out on us in sorrow and surprise,
For all men are of kin to one who dies.

IV.

   Eager the light grass bends
To let us pass, but springs again and waves
To hide our footsteps; not a flower saves
   Its blossoming, or sends
One odor less, as we go by;

And never seemed the shining sky
   So full of birds and songs before.
Whole tribes of yellow butterflies
   Dart mockingly and wheel and soar,
   Making it only seem the more
Impossible, this human death which lies
Silent beneath their dance who live
One day and die. Noiseless and swift,
Winged seeds come through the air, and drift
Down on the dead man's breast.
They shall go with him into rest,
And in the resurrection of the Spring
To his low grave shall give
The beauty of some green and flowering thing.

V.

The glittering sun moves slowly overhead,
It seems in rhythmic motion with our tread,
Confronting us with its relentless, hot,
   Unswerving, blinding ray;
     Then, sparing not
One subtle torture, it makes haste to lay
A ghastly shadow all along the way
Of formless, soundless wheel and lifeless plume,
All empty shapes in semblance of our gloom,
   Creeping along at our slow pace,
Not for one moment nor in any place
Forsaking us, nor ceasing to repeat
In taunting lines the faltering of our feet;
Laying, lifting, in a mocking breath,
Mocking shadows of the shadow of Death.

A FUNERAL MARCH.

VI.

But now comes silent joy, anointing
With sudden, firm, and tender hand
Our eyes; anointed with this clay
Of burial earth, we see how stand
Around us, marshalled under God's appointing,
Such shining ones as on no other day
Descend. We see, with a majestic face,
Of love ineffable, One walking in chief place
Beside the dead, — High Priest
  Of his salvation, King
Of his surrender, comrade till life ceased,
  Saviour from suffering, —
O sweet, strong, loving Death!
With yearning, pitying breath,
He looks back from his dead to us, and saith,
"O mine who love me not, what filled
Your hearts with this strange fear?
Could ye but hear
The new voice of this man whom I have willed
To set so free, to make
Him subject in my kingdom, for the sake
Of being greater king than I,
Reigning with Christ eternally!"

VII.

Closer and closer press the shining ones;
Clearer and clearer grow the notes
Of music from the heavenly throats.
We see the gleaming of the precious stones

Which set the Gate of Life. King's sons
Throng out to meet the man we bring;
We hear his voice in entering:
   "Oh! see how all these weep
   Who come with me!
   Must they return?
Oh! send swift messenger to Christ, and see
   If He will bid you keep
   Them too!"
      Scarce we discern
From distant Heaven where Christ sits and hears,
The tender whispered voice, in which he saith,
"My faithful servant, Death, is Lord of death:
My days must be a thousand years."

VIII.

The Gate of Life swings close. All have gone in;
Majestic Death, his freedman following;
And all those ghostly shapes, the next of kin,
Their deeds, which were and were not, rendering;
   And tender Joy and Grief,
   Bearing in one pale sheaf
Their harvest; and the shining ones who come
   And go continually.
   Alone and silently,
We take the road again that leads us home.
   The mother has no more a son;
The wife no husband; and the child
No father. Yet around the woman's days
Immortal loverhood lights blaze

Ot deathless fires; and never mother smiled
Like her who smiles forever, seeing one
Immortal child, for whom immortal fatherhood
Beseeches and receives eternal good.
And days that were not full are filled;
  And with triumphant breath,
  Mighty to cheer and save,
The voices ring which once were stilled,
The pulses beat which once were chilled,
  "Life is the victory of the grave,
Christ is Lord of the Lord of Death!"

JOY.

JOY, hast thou a shape?
  Hast thou a breath?
  How fillest thou the soundless air?
  Tell me the pillars of thy house!
What rest they on? Do they escape
  The victory of Death?
And are they fair
  Eternally, who enter in thy house?
O Joy, thou viewless spirit, canst thou dare
  To tell the pillars of thy house?

On adamant of pain,
  Before the earth
Was born of sea, before the sea,
Yea, and before the light, my house

Was built. None know what loss, what gain,
  Attends each travail birth.
No soul could be
  At peace when it had entered in my house,
If the foundations it could touch or see,
  Which stay the pillars of my house!

TWO TRUTHS.

"DARLING," he said, "I never meant
  To hurt you;" and his eyes were wet.
"I would not hurt you for the world:
  Am I to blame if I forget?"

"Forgive my selfish tears!" she cried,
  "Forgive! I knew that it was not
Because you meant to hurt me, sweet,—
  I knew it was that you forgot!"

But all the same, deep in her heart
  Rankled this thought, and rankles yet,—
"When love is at its best, one loves
  So much that he cannot forget."

GONDOLIEDS.

I.

YESTERDAY.

DEAR yesterday, glide not so fast;
    O, let me cling
To thy white garments floating past;
    Even to shadows which they cast
I cling, I cling.
    Show me thy face
Just once, once more; a single night
Cannot have brought a loss, a blight
    Upon its grace.

Nor are they dead whom thou dost bear,
    Robed for the grave.
See what a smile their red lips wear;
To lay them living wilt thou dare
    Into a grave?
    I know, I know,
I left thee first; now I repent;
I listen now; I never meant
    To have thee go.

Just once, once more, tell me the word
    Thou hadst for me!
Alas! although my heart was stirred,
I never fully knew or heard
    It was for me.
    O yesterday,

My yesterday, thy sorest pain,
Were joy couldst thou but come again, —
    Sweet yesterday.

Venice, May 26.

II.

TO-MORROW.

All red with joy the waiting west,
    O little swallow,
Couldst thou tell me which road is best?
Cleaving high air with thy soft breast
    For keel, O swallow,
    Thou must o'erlook
My seas and know if I mistake;
I would not the same harbor make
    Which yesterday forsook.

I hear the swift blades dip and plash
    Of unseen rowers;
On unknown land the waters dash;
Who knows how it be wise or rash
    To meet the rowers!
    Premì! Premì!
Venetia's boatmen lean and cry;
With voiceless lips, I drift and lie
    Upon the twilight sea.

The swallow sleeps. Her last low call
    Had sound of warning.

"SPOKEN."

Sweet little one, whate'er befall,
Thou wilt not know that it was all,
    In vain thy warning.
    I may not borrow
A hope, a help. I close my eyes;
Cold wind blows from the Bridge of Sighs;
Kneeling I wait to-morrow.

VENICE, May 30.

"SPOKEN."

COUNTING the hours by bells and lights
    We rose and sank;
The waves on royal banquet-heights
    Tossed off and drank
Their jewels made of sun and moon,
White pearls at midnight, gold at noon.

    Counting the hours by bells and lights,
        We sailed and sailed;
Six lonely days, six lonely nights,
    No ship we hailed.
Till all the sea seemed bound in spell,
And silence sounded like a knell.

    At last, just when by bells and lights
        Of seventh day
The dawn grew clear, in sudden flights
        White sails away

To east, like birds, went spreading slow
Their wings which reddened in the glow.

No more we count the bells and lights;
    We laugh for joy.
The trumpets with their brazen mights
    Call, "Ship ahoy!"
We hold each other's hands; our cheeks
Are wet with tears; but no one speaks.

In instant comes the sun and lights
    The ship with fire;
Each mast creeps up to dizzy heights,
    A blazing spire;
One faint "Ahoy," then all in vain
We look; we are alone again.

I have forgotten bells and lights,
    And waves which drank
Their jewels up; those days and nights
    Which rose and sank
Have turned like other pasts, and fled,
And carried with them all their dead.

But every day that fire ship lights
    My distant blue,
And every day glad wonder smites
    My heart anew,
How in that instant each could heed
And hear the other's swift God-speed.

Counting by hours thy days and nights
    In weariness,
O patient soul, on godlike heights
    Of loneliness,
I passed thee by; tears filled our eyes;
The loud winds mocked and drowned our cries.

The hours go by, with bells and lights;
    We sail, we drift;
Our souls in changing tasks and rites,
    Find work and shrift.
But this I pray, and praying know
Till faith almost to joy can grow

That hour by hour the bells, the lights
    Of sound of flame
Weave spell which ceaselessly recites
    To thee a name,
And smiles which thou canst not forget
For thee are suns which never set.

THE WAY TO SING.

THE birds must know. Who wisely sings
    Will sing as they;
The common air has generous wings
    Songs make their way.

No messenger to run before,
    Devising plan ;
No mention of the place or hour
    To any man ;
No waiting till some sound betrays
    A listening ear ;
No different voice, no new delays,
    If steps draw near.

"What bird is that?　Its song is good."
    And eager eyes
Go peering through the dusky wood,
    In glad surprise.
Then late at night, when by his fire
    The traveller sits,
Watching the flame grow brighter, higher,
    The sweet song flits
By snatches through his weary brain
    To help him rest ;
When next he goes that road again,
    An empty nest
On leafless bough will make him sigh,
    "Ah me ! last spring
Just here I heard, in passing by,
    That rare bird sing ! "

But while he sighs, remembering
    How sweet the song,
The little bird on tireless wing,
    Is borne along

In other air, and other men
   With weary feet,
On other roads, the simple strain
   Are finding sweet.
The birds must know. Who wisely sings
   Will sing as they;
The common air has generous wings,
   Songs make their way.

THE TRUE BALLAD OF THE KING'S SINGER.

THE king rode fast, the king rode well,
   The royal hunt went loud and gay,
A thousand bleeding chamois fell
   For royal sport that day.

When sunset turned the hills all red,
   The royal hunt went still and slow;
The king's great horse with weary tread
   Plunged ankle-deep in snow.

Sudden a strain of music sweet,
   Unearthly sweet, came through the wood;
Up sprang the king, and on both feet
   Straight in his saddle stood.

" Now, by our lady, be it bird,
　Or be it man or elf who plays,
Never before my ears have heard
　A music fit for praise ! "

Sullen and tired, the royal hunt
　Followed the king, who tracked the song,
Unthinking, as is royal wont,
　How hard the way and long.

Stretched on a rock the shepherd lay
　And dreamed and piped, and dreamed and sang,
And careless heard the shout and bay
　With which the echoes rang.

" Up, man ! the king ! " the hunters cried.
　He slowly stood, and, wondering,
Turned honest eyes from side to side :
　To him, each looked like king.

Strange shyness seized the king's bold tongue ;
　He saw how easy to displease
This savage man who stood among
　His courtiers, so at ease.

But kings have silver speech to use
　When on their pleasure they are bent ;
The simple shepherd could not choose ;
　Like one in dream he went.

O hear ! O hear !　The ringing sound
　Of twenty trumpets swept the street,

The king a minstrel now has found,
   For royal music meet.

With cloth of gold, and cloth of red,
   And woman's eyes the place is bright.
"Now, shepherd, sing," the king has said,
   "The song you sang last night!"

One faint sound stirs the perfumed air,
   The courtiers scornfully look down;
The shepherd kneels in dumb despair,
   Seeing the king's dark frown.

The king is just; the king will wait.
   "Ho, guards! let him be gently led,
Let him grow used to royal state, —
   To being housed and fed."

All night the king unquiet lay,
   Racked by his dream's presentiment;
Then rose in haste at break of day,
   And for the shepherd sent.

"Ho now, thou beast, thou savage man,
   How sound thou sleepest, not to hear!"
They jeering laughed, but soon began
   To louder call in fear.

They wrenched the bolts; unrumpled stood
   The princely bed all silken fine,
Untouched the plates of royal food,
   The flask of royal wine!

The costly robes strewn on the floor,
  The chamber empty, ghastly still;
The guards stood trembling at the door,
  And dared not cross the sill.

All night the sentinels their round
  Had kept. No man could pass that way.
The window dizzy high from ground;
  Below, the deep moat lay.

They crossed themselves. "The foul fiend lurks
  In this," they said. They did not know
The miracles sweet Freedom works,
  To let her children go.

It was the fiend himself who took
  That shepherd's shape to pipe and sing;
And every man with terror shook,
  For who would tell the king!

The heads of men all innocent
  Rolled in the dust that day;
And east and west the bloodhounds went,
  Baying their dreadful bay;

Safe on a snow too far, too high,
  For scent of dogs or feet of men,
The shepherd watched the clouds sail by,
  And dreamed and sang again;

And crossed himself, and knelt and cried,
  And kissed the holy Edelweiss,

Believing that the fiends had tried
    To buy him with a price.

The king rides fast, the king rides well;
    The summer hunts go loud and gay;
The courtiers, who this tale can tell,
    Are getting old and gray.

But still they say it was a fiend
    That took a shepherd's shape to sing,
For still the king's heart is not weaned
    To care for other thing.

Great minstrels come from far and near,
    He will not let them sing or play,
But waits and listens still to hear
    The song he heard that day.

ŒNONE.

WOE to thee, Œnone! stricken blind
And poisoned by a darkness and a pain,
O, woe to thee, Œnone! who couldst find
No love when love lay dying, doubly slain
Slain thus by thee, Œnone!
                O, what stain,
Of red like this on hands of love was seen
Ever before or since, since love has been!

O, woe to thee, Œnone ! Hadst thou said,
" Sweet love, lost love, I know now why I live
And could not die, the days I wished me dead;
O love, all strength of life and joy I give
Thee back ! Ah me, that I have dared to strive
With fates that bore me to this one sure bliss,
Thou couldst not rob me, O lost love, of this ? " —

Hadst thou said this, Œnone, though he went
Bounding with life, thy life, and left thee there
Dying and glad, such sudden pain had rent
His heart, that even beating in the fair
White arms of Helen, hid in her sweet hair,
It had made always moan, in strange unrest,
" Œnone's love was greater love, was best."

[" Paris, the son of Priam, was wounded by one of the poisoned arrows of Hercules that Philoctetes bore to the siege of Troy, whereupon he had himself borne up into Ida, that he might see the nymph Œnone, whom he once had loved, because she who knew many secret things alone could heal him; but when he had seen her and spoken with her, she would deal with the matter in no wise, whereupon Paris died of that hurt."]

THE LONELINESS OF SORROW.

FRIENDS crowd around and take it by the hand,
Intruding gently on its loneliness,
Striving with word of love and sweet caress
To draw it into light and air. Like band
Of brothers, all men gather close, and stand
About it, making half its grief their own,
Leaving it never silent nor alone.

But through all crowds of strangers and of friends,
Among all voices of good-will and cheer,
Walks Sorrow, silently, and does not hear.
Like hermit whom mere loneliness defends;
Like one born deaf, to whose still ear sound sends
No word of message; and like one born dumb,
From whose sealed lips complaint can never come.

Majestic in its patience, and more sweet
Than all things else that can of souls have birth,
Bearing the one redemption of this earth
Which God's eternities fulfil, complete,
Down to its grave, with steadfast, tireless feet,
It goes uncomforted, serene, alone,
And leaves not even name on any stone.

A SUNRISE.

HE slept on a bed of roses,
                I know —
  I, who am least of his subjects. The thing
Chanced thus.
           Before it was time for the king
To rise — just before — I saw a red glow
Stream out of his door, such as roses show
At heart, such a glow as no fire could bring.
The solid gold of the whole eastern wing
Of the palace seemed pale.
          Then, floating low
Across the threshold, great petals of pink
Fell from the feet of the king, as he stood
There, smiling, majestic, serene, and good.
But was it a bed of roses?
              I think
Of another monarch who, on the brink
Of death by fire, smiled, as a monarch should

A BALLAD OF THE GOLD COUNTRY.

EEP in the hill the gold sand burned;
    The brook ran yellow with its gleams;
Close by, the seekers slept, and turned
    And tossed in restless dreams.

At dawn they waked. In friendly cheer
    Their dreams they told, by one, by one;
And each man laughed the dreams to hear,
    But sighed when they were done.

Visions of golden birds that flew,
    Of golden cloth piled fold on fold,
Of rain which shone, and filtered through
    The air in showers of gold;

Visions of golden bells that rang,
    Of golden chariots that rolled,
Visions of girls that danced and sang,
    With hair and robes of gold;

Visions of golden stairs that led
    Down golden shafts of depths untold,
Visions of golden skies that shed
    Gold light on seas of gold.

"Comrades, your dreams have many shapes,"
  Said one who, thoughtful, sat apart:
"But I six nights have dreamed of grapes,
  One dream which fills my heart.

"A woman meets me, crowned with vine;
  Great purple clusters fill her hands;
Her eyes divinely smile and shine,
  As beckoning she stands.

"I follow her a single pace;
  She vanishes, like light or sound,
And leaves me in a vine-walled place,
  Where grapes pile all the ground."

The comrades laughed: "We know thee by
  This fevered, drunken dream of thine."
"Ha, ha," cried he, "never have I
  So much as tasted wine!

"Now, follow ye your luring shapes
  Of gold that clinks and gold that shines;
I shall await my maid of grapes,
  And plant her trees and vines."

All through the hills the gold sand burned;
  All through the lands ran yellow streams;
To right, to left, the seekers turned,
  Led by the golden gleams.

The ruddy hills were gulfed and strained;
  The rocky fields were torn and trenched;
The yellow streams were drained and drained,
  Until their sources quenched.

The gold came fast; the gold came free:
  The seekers shouted as they ran,
"Now let us turn aside, and see
  How fares that husbandman!"

"Ho here! ho there! good man," they cried,
  And tossed gold nuggets at his feet;
"Serve us with wine! Where is thy bride
  That told thee tales so sweet?"

"No wine as yet, my friends, to sell;
  No bride to show," he smiling said:
"But here is water from my well;
  And here is wheaten bread."

"Is this thy tale?" they jeering cried;
  "Who was it followed luring shapes?
And who has won? It seems she lied,
  Thy maid of purple grapes!"

"When years have counted up to ten,"
  He answered gayly, smiling still,
"Come back once more, my merry men,
  And you shall have your fill

"Of purple grapes and sparkling wine,
    And figs, and nectarines like flames,
And sweeter eyes than maids' shall shine
    In welcome at your names."

In scorn they heard; to scorn they laughed
    The water and the wheaten bread;
"We'll wait until a better draught
    For thy bride's health," they said.

.   .   .   .   .

The years ran fast. The seekers went
    All up, all down the golden lands:
The streams grew pale; the hills were spent;
    Slow ran the golden sands.

And men were beggars in a day,
    For swift to come was swift to go;
What chance had got, chance flung away
    On one more chance's throw.

And bleached and seamed and riven plains,
    And tossed and tortured rocks like ghosts,
And blackened lines and charred remains,
    And crumbling chimney-posts,

For leagues their ghastly records spread
    Of youth, and years, and fortunes gone,
Like graveyards whose sad living dead
    Had hopeless journeyed on.

.   .   .   .   .   .

The years had counted up to ten :
    One night, as it grew chill and late,
The husbandman marked beggar-men
    Who leaned upon his gate.

" Ho here ! good men," he eager cried,
    Before the wayfarers could speak ;
" This is my vineyard.   Far and wide,
    For laborers I seek.

" This year has doubled on last year;
    The fruit breaks down my vines and trees ;
Tarry and help, till wine runs clear,
    And ask what price you please."

Purple and red, to left, to right,
    For miles the gorgeous vintage blazed;
And all day long and into night
    The vintage song was raised.

And wine ran free all thirst beyond,
    And no hand stinted bread or meat ;
And maids were gay, and men were fond,
    And hours were swift and sweet.

The beggar-men they worked with will;
    Their hands were thin and lithe and strong:
Each day they ate good two days' fill,
    They had been starved so long.

The vintage drew to end. New wine
   From thousand casks was dripping slow,
And bare and yellow fields gave sign
   For vintagers to go.

The beggar-men received their pay,
   Bright yellow gold, — twice their demand;
The master, as they turned away,
   Held out his brawny hand,

And said: "Good men, this time next year
   My vintage will be bigger still;
Come back, if chance should bring you near,
   And it should suit your will."

The beggars nodded. But at night
   They said: "No more we go that way:
He did not know us then; he might
   Upon another day!"

EXILE.

MEN may be banished, and a blood-price
  set,
  Tracking their helpless steps in every
      land,
Arming against their life each base man's hand,
But light and air and memory are met
In holy league, to help and save them yet,
From all of death which souls cannot withstand:
The subtlest cruelty which ever planned,
Can never make them pray they may forget
Because they are forgotten.
                           They may go,
Driven of earth and tossed by salt sea's foam,
Till every breath one slow dull pain become;
It is not exile. Only exiles know: .
Nor distance makes, nor nearness saves the blow;
The exile had of exile died at home.

MY SHIP.

MY brothers' ships sail out by night, by day;
  My brothers' feet run merry on the shore,
  They need not weep, believing they no
      more
Shall find the loved ones who have sailed away,

So frequent go their ships, to-morrow may
See one return for them.
                    The ship that bore
My loved from me lies where she lay before ;
My heart grows sick within me as I pray
The silent skipper, morn by morn, if he
Will sail before the night.
                    With patient tread
I bear him all my goods. I cannot see
What more is left that could be stripped from me,
But still the silent skipper shakes his head :
Ah me ! I think I never shall be dead !

AT LAST.

THE years I lost before I knew you,
          Love !
O, the hills I climbed and came not to you,
          Love !
Ah ! who shall render unto us to make
          Us glad,
The things which for and of each other's sake
          We might have had ?

If you and I had sat and played together,
          Love,
Two speechless babies in the summer weather,
          Love,

AT LAST.

By one sweet brook which, though it dried up long
      Ago,
Still makes for me to-day a sweeter song
      Than all I know, —

If hand in hand through the mysterious gateway,
      Love,
Of womanhood, we had first looked and straightway,
      Love,
Had whispered to each other softly, ere
      It yet
Was dawn, what now in noonday heat and fear
      We both forget, —

If all of this had given its completeness,
      Love,
To every hour would it be added sweetness,
      Love?
Could I know sooner whether it were well
      Or ill
With thee? One wish could I more surely tell,
      More swift fulfil?

Ah! vainly thus I sit and dream and ponder,
      Love,
Losing the precious present while I wonder,
      Love,
About the days in which you grew and came
      To be
So beautiful, and did not know the name
      Or sight of me.

But all lost things are in the angels' keeping,
  Love ;
No past is dead for us, but only sleeping,
  Love ;
The years of Heaven will all earth's little pain
  Make good,
Together there we can begin again
  In babyhood.

MEMOIR OF A QUEEN.

HER name, before she was a queen, boots
  not.
 When she was crowned, her kingdom said,
  " The Queen ! "
And, after that, all other names too mean
By far had seemed. Perhaps all were forgot,
Save " Queen, sweet queen."
      Such pitiable lot
As till her birth her kingdom had, was seen
Never in all fair lands, so torn between
False grasping powers, that toiled and fought, but got
No peace. All curious search is wholly vain
For written page or stone whereon occurs
A mention of the kingdom which obeyed
This sweet queen's rule. But centuries have laid
No dead queen down in royal sepulchres
Whose reign was greater or more blest than hers.

OUR ANGELS.

AH ! not with any sound they come, or sign,
    Which fleshly ear or eye can recognize;
    No curiosity can compass or surprise
The secret of that intercourse divine
Which God permits, ordains, across the line,
    The changeless line which bars
    Our earth from other stars.

But they do come and go continually,
    Our blessed angels, no less ours than His ;
    The blessed angels whom we think we miss ;
Whose empty graves we weep to name or see,
And vainly watch, as once in Galilee
    One, weeping, watched in vain,
    Where her lost Christ had lain.

Whenever in some bitter grief we find,
    All unawares, a deep, mysterious sense
    Of hidden comfort come, we know not whence ;
When suddenly we see, where we were blind ;
Where we had struggled, are content, resigned ;
    Are strong where we were weak, —
    And no more strive nor seek, —

Then we may know that from the far glad skies,
    To note our need, the watchful God has bent,
    And for our instant help has called and sent,

Of all our loving angels, the most wise
And tender one, to point to us where lies
    The path that will be best,
    The path of peace and rest.

And when we find on every sky and field
   A sudden, new, and mystic light, which fills
   Our every sense with speechless joy, and thrills
Us, till we yield ourselves as children yield
Themselves and watch the spells magicians wield,
    With tireless, sweet surprise,
    And rapture in their eyes, —

Then we may know our little ones have run
   Away for just one moment, from their play
   In heavenly gardens, and in their old way
Are walking by our side, and one by one,
At all sweet things beneath the earthly sun,
    Are pointing joyfully,
    And calling us to see!

Ah! when we learn the spirit sound and sign,
   And instantly our angels recognize,
   No weariness can tire, no pain surprise
Our souls rapt in the intercourse divine,
Which God permits, ordains, across the line,
    The changeless line which bars
    Our earth from other stars.

MAZZINI.

THAT he is dead the sons of kings are glad;
And in their beds the tyrants sounder sleep.
Now he is dead his martyrdom will reap
   Late harvest of the palms it should have had
In life. Too late the tardy lands are sad.
His unclaimed crown in secret they will keep
For ages, while in chains they vainly weep,
And vainly grope to find the roads he bade
Them take.
   O glorious soul! there is no dearth
Of worlds. There must be many better worth
Thy presence and thy leadership than this.
No doubt, on some great sun to-day, thy birth
Is for a race, the dawn of Freedom's bliss,
Which but for thee it might for ages miss.

"WHEN THE TIDE COMES IN."

WHEN the tide comes in,
   At once the shore and sea begin
   Together to be glad.
   What the tide has brought
No man has asked, no man has sought:

What other tides have had
The deep sand hides away;
The last bit of the wrecks they wrought
Was burned up yesterday.

When the tide goes out,
The shore looks dark and sad with doubt.
The landmarks are all lost.
For the tide to turn
Men patient wait, men restless yearn.
Sweet channels they have crossed,
In boats that rocked with glee,
Stretch now bare stony roads that burn
And lead away from sea.

When the tide comes in
In hearts, at once the hearts begin
Together to be glad.
What the tide has brought
They do not care, they have not sought.
All joy they ever had
The new joy multiplies;
All pain by which it may be bought
Seems paltry sacrifice.

When the tide goes out,
The hearts are wrung with fear and doubt:
All trace of joy seems lost.
Will the tide return?
In restless questioning they yearn,

With hands unclasped, uncrossed,
    They weep, on separate ways.
Ah! darling, shall we ever learn
    Love's tidal hours and days?

THE SINGER'S HILLS.

HE dwelt where level lands lay low and drear,
    Long stretches of waste meadow pale and
    sere,
With dull seas languid tiding up and down,
Turning the lifeless sands from white to brown,—
Wide barren fields for miles and miles, until
The pale horizon walled them in, and still
No lifted peak, no slope, not even mound
To raise and cheer the weary eye was found.
From boyhood up and down these dismal lands,
And pacing to and fro the barren sands,
And always gazing, gazing seaward, went
The Singer. Daily with the sad winds blent
His yearning voice.
                "There must be hills," he said,
"I know they stand at sunset rosy red,
And purple in the dewy shadowed morn;
Great forest trees like babes are rocked and borne
Upon their breasts, and flowers like jewels shine
Around their feet, and gold and silver line

Their hidden chambers, and great cities rise
Stately where their protecting shadow lies,
And men grow brave and women are more fair
'Neath higher skies, and in the clearer air!"
One day thus longing, gazing, lo! in awe
Made calm by ecstasy, he sudden saw,
Far out to seaward, mountain peaks appear,
Slow rising from the water pale and clear.
Purple and azure, there they were, as he
Had faithful yearning visions they must be;
Purple and azure and bright rosy red,
Like flashing jewels, on the sea they shed
Their quenchless light.
     Great tears ran down
The Singer's cheeks, and through the busy town,
And all across the dreary meadow lands,
And all along the dreary lifeless sands,
He called aloud,
    "Ho! tarry! tarry ye!
Behold those purple mountains in the sea!"
The people saw no mountains!
      "He is mad,"
They careless said, and went their way and had
No farther thought of him.
      And so, among
His fellows' noisy, idle, crowding throng,
The Singer walked, as strangers walk who speak
A foreign tongue and have no friend to seek.
And yet the silent joy which filled his face
Sometimes their wonder stirred a little space,
And following his constant seaward look,
One wistful gaze they also seaward took.

One day the Singer was not seen. Men said
That as the early day was breaking red,
He rowed far out to sea, rowed swift and strong,
Toward the spot where he had gazed so long.
Then all the people shook their heads, and went
A little sadly, thinking he had spent
His life in vain, and sorry they no more
Should hear his sweet mad songs along their shore.
But when the sea with sunset hues was dyed,
A boat came slowly drifting with the tide,
Nor oar nor rudder set to turn or stay,
And on the crimson deck the Singer lay.
"Ah, he is dead," some cried. "No! he but sleeps,"
Said others, "madman that he is, joy keeps
Sweet vigils with him now."
      The light keel grazed
The sands; alert and swift the Singer raised
His head, and with red cheeks and eyes aflame
Leaped out, and shouted loud, and called by name
Each man, and breathlessly his story told.
"Lo, I have landed on the hills of gold!
See, these are flowers, and these are fruits, and these
Are boughs from off the giant forest trees;
And these are jewels which lie loosely there,
And these are stuffs which beauteous maidens wear!"
And staggering he knelt upon the sands
As laying burdens down.
      But empty hands
His fellows saw, and passed on smiling. Yet,
The ecstasy in which his face was set
Again smote on their hearts with sudden sense
Of half involuntary reverence.

And some said, whispering, " Alack, is he
The madman ?   Have ye never heard there be
Some spells which make men blind ? "
                                And thenceforth they
More closely watched the Singer day by day,
Till finally they said, " He is not mad.
There be such hills, and treasure to be had
For seeking there ! We too without delay
Will sail."
            And of the men who sailed that way,
Some found the purple mountains in the sea,
Landed, and roamed their treasure countries free,
And drifted back with brimming laden hands.
Walking along the lifeless silent sands,
The Singer, gazing ever seaward, knew,
Well knew the odors which the soft wind blew
Of all the fruits and flowers and boughs they bore.
Standing with hands stretched eager on the shore,
When they leaped out, he called, " Now God be praised,
Sweet comrades, were they then not fair ? "
                                        Amazed,
And with dull scorn, the other men who brought
No treasures, found no mountains, and saw naught
In these men's hands, beheld them kneeling low,
Lifting, shouting, and running to and fro
As men unlading argosies whose freight
Of gorgeous things bewildered by its weight.

   Tireless the great years waxed; the great years
        waned ;
Slowly the Singer's comrades grew and gained

THE SINGER'S HILLS.

Till they were goodly number.
                              No man's scorn
Could hurt or hinder them.   No pity born
Of it could make them blush, or once make less
Their joy's estate ; and as for loneliness
They knew it not.
                    Still rise the magic hills,
Purple and gold and red ; the shore still thrills
With fragrance when the sunset winds begin
To blow and waft the subtle odors in
From treasure laden boats that drift, and bide
The hours and moments of the wave and tide,
Laden with fruits and boughs and flowers rare,
And jewels such as monarchs do not wear,
And costly stuffs which dazzle on the sight,
Stuffs wrought for purest virgin, bravest knight ;
And men with cheeks all red, and eyes aflame,
And hearts that call to hearts by brothers' name,
Still leap out on the silent lifeless sands,
And staggering with over-burdened hands
Joyous lay down the treasures they have brought,
While smiling, pitying, the world sees nought !

COVERT.

NE day, when sunny fields lay warm and still,
   And from their tufted hillocks, thick and sweet
    With moss and pine and ferns, such spicy heat
Rose up, it seemed the air to over-fill,
And quicken every sense with subtle thrill,
   I rambled on with careless, aimless feet,
   And lingered idly, finding all so sweet.

Sudden, almost beneath my footsteps' weight,
   Almost before the sunny silence heard
   Their sound, from a low bush, which scarcely stirred
A twig at lightening of its hidden freight,
Flew, frightened from her nest, the small brown mate
   Of some melodious, joyous, soaring bird,
   Whose song that instant high in air I heard.

  .   .   .   .

"Ah! Heart," I said, "when days are warm and sweet,
   And sunny hours for very joy are still,
   And every sense feels subtle, languid thrill
Of voiceless memory's renewing heat,
Fly not at sound of strangers' aimless feet!
   Of thy love's distant song drink all thy fill!
   Thy hiding-place is safe. Glad heart, keep still!"

WAITING.

I KNOW it will not be to-day;
   I know it will not be to-morrow;
   Oh, half in joy and half in sorrow,
   I watch the slow swift hours away;
I bid them haste, then bid them stay,
   I long so for the coming day.

   I long so, I would rather wait;
Each hour I see the unseen comer;
Each hour turns ripe in secret summer
   The joys which I anticipate.
   O precious feet, come slow, come late!
   I long so, it is bliss to wait!

   Ah, sweet sad life, so far to-day!
Ah, sweet sad life, so near to-morrow!
Can joy be joy when we miss sorrow?
   When earth's last sun has rolled away
   In tideless time, and we can say
   No more, "To-morrow," or "To-day"?

RENUNCIATION.

WHEREFORE thus, apart with droop-
    ing wings
  Thou stillest, saddest angel,
  With hidden face, as if but bitter things
Thou hadst, and no evangel
Of good tidings?

Thou know'st that through our tears
  Of hasty, selfish weeping,
Comes surer sun; and for our petty fears
  Of loss, thou hast in keeping
A greater gain than all of which we dreamed.
  Thou knowest that in grasping
The bright possessions which so precious seemed,
  We lose them; but, if clasping
Thy faithful hand, we tread with steadfast feet
  The path of thy appointing,
There waits for us a treasury of sweet
  Delight; royal anointing
With oil of gladness and of strength!
                        O, things
  Of Heaven, Christ's evangel
Bearing, call us with shining face and poised wings,
  Thou sweetest, dearest angel!

BURNT SHIPS.

 LOVE, sweet Love, who came with rosy
sail
And foaming prow across the misty sea!
O Love, brave Love, whose faith was full
and free
That lands of sun and gold, which could not fail,
Lay in the west, that bloom no wintry gale
Could blight, and eyes whose love thine own should
be,
Called thee, with steadfast voice of prophecy,
To shores unknown!
O Love, poor Love, avail
Thee nothing now thy faiths, thy braveries;
There is no sun, no bloom; a cold wind strips
The bitter foam from off the wave where dips
No more thy prow; the eyes are hostile eyes;
The gold is hidden; vain thy tears and cries;
O Love, poor Love, why didst thou burn thy ships?

RESURGAM.

NOW, still, unutterably weak,
    In human helplessness more helpless than
    The smallest of God's other creatures can
    Be left, I lie and do not speak.
  Walls rise and close
  Around. No warning shows
To me, who am but blind, which wall
Will shelter, and which one will fall
    And crush me in the dust,
    Not that I sinned, but that it must.
Each hour, within my heart, some sweet hope
    dies.
Each night the dead form lies
Of some fair purpose which I could not save,
    Ready for day to carry out and hide
    In a dishonored grave.
    My strongest will
Finds stronger fate stand side by side
With it, its utmost efforts conquering still
With such swift might, the dust in which I lie
Scarce quivers with my struggle and my pain,
    Scarce echoes with my cry.
    Grief comes and passes by,
    And Joy comes hand in hand
With Grief, each bearing crowns with buds of
    snow,
Both laying crowns upon my head.
  Soon as the buds are open, it were vain
To try to separate or understand —

No sense of mine can feel or know —
Which flowers the hand of Joy has shed,
  And which the hand of Pain.
    Therefore I do not choose;
  Fearing, desiring equally from each,
    I wait. I do not dare refuse.
    Only one sound can reach
Me where I lie, can stir my veins,
    Or make me lift my eyes.
    That sound drops from the skies,
A still small voice, — round it great silence lies:
"Not one of all these things remains.
    Thou shalt arise!"

    Somewhere on earth,
Marked, sealed, mine from its hour of birth,
A stairway lies, down which I shall descend,
And pass through a dark gate, which at my
    name,
  And at no other, will swing back and close.
  Where lies this stairway no man knows,
  No man has even wondered. Only I
    Remember it continually.
    Spring never came,
Her grasses setting, that I did not bend
Low in the fields, saying: "Lend
But part trust, O Summer! Many graves,
Before this sweet grass waves
Half grown, must open. Ah! will reapers reap
  Harvest from my low resting-place
This year? Or will the withered sods and I

   Lifeless together lie,
  With silent, upturned face,
Before the autumn winds sweep by?"
   And when the winter snows lie deep,
  I think: "How hard to find,
Just now, those hidden stairs that wind
For me." The time must near the end.
Perhaps for those I leave behind,
More sad to see the snow. But its pure white,
I think, would shed a little light,
  And stretch like alabaster skies
Above the stairway dark I must descend,
   That I may rise.

   Somewhere on earth,
Marked, sealed, mine from its hour of birth,
   There lies a shining stone,
    My own.
Perhaps it still is in the quarry's hold.
Oh! Pine Tree, wave in winter's cold
Swifter above it; in the summer's heat
Drop spices on it, thick and sweet;
Quicken its patient crystals' growth.
   Oh! be not loth,
   Quarry and Pine,
And stir of birds in the still North,
   And suns that shine, —
Give up my smooth white stone! Hasten it forth.
  My soul in bondage lies.
   I must arise.

RESURGAM.

Perhaps upon the shining stone,
        My own,
Even to-day the hammers ring.
The workman does not sing.
He is a lover and he has a child ;
To him a gravestone is a fearful thing.
    He has not smiled
Since under his strong hands the white stone
    came,
    Though he is slow and dull,
    And could not give a name
To thoughts which fill his heart too full
    Of prophecy and pain.
O Workman, sing ! See how the white dust flies
    And glistens in the sunny air.
    No grain but counts ;
Some fair spot grows more fair
By it, each moment. In the skies,
    My moment must be near.
Workman, there is on earth no loss, no waste.
    Sing loud, and make all haste ;
        I must arise.

Perhaps even now the shining stone,
        My own,
Stands ready, — arch and base,
And chiselled lines, and space
For name all done : and yesterday
Some sorrowing ones stood round it silently,
    And looked at it through tears,
    But passed it by,

Saying, with trembling lips: "No, no!
For stone more beautiful than this we seek.
　Sculptor, dost thou not know
　　What lines will make the marble show
　　　A deeper grief?" Ah! mourners, speak
　　In lower voice. Ye do not see
　　　　What presence guards
The stone. More than ye dream retards
Your will. The stone waits there for me.
　My soul in bondage lies.
　　　　I must arise.

Then, when I have descended, and the stone
　Above the stairway has been set,
The tears of those who reckoned me their own
　A little space will wet
The grass; but soon all saddened days
Count up to comforted and busy years:
All living men must go their ways
And leave their dead behind. The tideless light
Of sun and moon and stars,—silence of night
And noise of day, and whirling of the great
　　　Round world itself,—yea,
All things which are and are not work to lay
　　　The dead away.
The crumbling of the stone, more late,
The sinking of the little mound
To unmarked level, where with noisy sound
Roam idle and unwitting feet,
Least tokens are and smallest part
　　　Of the oblivion complete

Which wraps a human grave;
And unto me, the hour when the last heart
    Has ceased to save
    My memory, the year
That sees my white stone lying low,
The century that sees the grave mound grow,
Free of my dust, to solid earth again,
Made ready for new dead, — all these will be
    Alike to me,
    Alike uncounted will remain.
    Their sound I shall not hear
    As I arise.
They mark no moments in the skies
Through which I mount. As constant as
    God's law,
Bearing all joy and grief my first years saw,
    Even my babyhood, —
    Bearing all evil and all good
    Of ripest age, — nowise
    Escaping and nowise forgetting one
    Of all the actions done, —
    And bearing all that lies
In utmost law for me, — all God's great will,
All God's great mercy, — still
    I shall arise.

The fool asks, "With what flesh? in joy or pain?
Helped or unhelped? and lonely, or again
   Surrounded by our earthly friends?"
I know not; and I glory that I do
   Not know: that for Eternity's great ends

God counted me as worthy of such trust,
    That I need not be told.
        I hold
      That if it be
Less than enough to any soul to know
Itself immortal, immortality
In all its boundless spaces will not find
     A place designed
      So small, so low,
That to a fitting home such soul can go.
    Out to the earthward brink
    Of that great tideless sea
Light from Christ's garments streams.
Cowards who fear to tread such beams
The angels can but pity when they sink.
  Believing thus, I joy although I lie in dust.
    I joy, not that I ask or choose,
  But simply that I must.
    I love and fear not; and I cannot lose,
One instant, this great certainty of peace.
Long as God ceases not, I cannot cease;
    I must arise.

THE VILLAGE LIGHTS.

ONLY a little village street,
　　Lying along a mountain's side;
Only the silences which meet
　　When weary hands and weary feet
By night's sweet rest are satisfied;
Only the dark of summer nights;
Only the commonest of sights,
The glimmer of the village lights!

I know not, then, why it should bring
　　Into my eyes such sudden tears.
But to the mountain's sheltering
The little village seems to cling,
　　As child, all unaware of fears,
Unconscious that it is caressed,
In perfect peace and perfect rest
Asleep upon its mother's breast.

No stir, no sound! The shadows creep.
　　The old and young, in common trust,
Are lying down to wait, asleep,
While Life and Joy will come to keep
　　With Death and Pain what tryst they must.
O faith! for faith almost too great!
Come slow, O day of evil freight!
O village hearts, sleep well, sleep late!

TRANSPLANTED.

WHEN Christ, the Gardener, said, "These
    many years
      Behold how I have waited
        For fruit upon this barren tree, which bears
But leaves! With unabated
Patience I have nurtured it; have fed
    Its roots with choicest juices;
The sweetest suns their tender warmth have shed
    On it; still it refuses
Its blossom; all the balmiest summer rain
    Has bathed it; unrepaying,
Still, its green and glittering leaves, in vain
    And empty show arraying,
It flaunts, contented in its uselessness,
    Ever my eye offending.
Uproot it! Set it in the wilderness!
    There no more gentle tending
Shall it receive; but, pricked by nettle stings,
    And bruised and hurt, and crowded
By stones, and weeds, and noxious growths of things
    That kill, and chilled 'neath shrouded
And sunless skies, from whose black clouds no rain
    Shall fall to soothe its anguish,
Bearing the utmost it can feel of pain,
    Unsuccored, it shall languish!"

When next across the wilderness Christ came,
    Seeking his Royal Garden,

TRANSPLANTED.

A tree stood in his pathway, all aflame,
    And bending with its burden
Of burnished gold. No fruit inside the wall
    Had grown to such perfection!
It was the outcast tree! Deprived of all
    Kind nurture and protection,
Thrust out among vile things of poisonous growth,
    Condemned, disgraced, and banished,
Lonely and scorned, its energies put forth
    Anew. All false show vanished;
Its roots struck downward with determined hold,
    No more the surface roaming;
And from th' unfriendly soil, a thousand-fold
    Of yield compelled.
                  The coming
Of the Gardener now in sweet humility
    It waited. trusting, trembling;
Then Christ, the Gardener, smiled and said:
                    "O tree,
This day, in the assembling
    Of mine, in Paradise, shalt thou be found.
        Henceforth in me abiding,
More golden fruit shalt thou bring forth; and round
    Thy root the living waters gliding
Shall give the greenness which can never fade.
While angels, with thy new name sealing
    Thee, shall come, and gather in thy shade
Leaves for the nations' healing!"

BEST.

MOTHER, I see you with your nursery light,
   Leading your babies, all in white,
      To their sweet rest ;
   Christ, the Good Shepherd, carries mine to-night,
      And that is best.

I cannot help tears, when I see them twine
Their fingers in yours, and their bright curls shine
      On your warm breast ;
But the Saviour's is purer than yours or mine,
      He can love best !

You tremble each hour because your arms
Are weak ; your heart is wrung with alarms,
      And sore opprest ;
My darlings are safe, out of reach of harms,
      And that is best.

You know, over yours may hang even now
Pain and disease, whose fulfilling slow
      Naught can arrest ;
Mine in God's gardens run to and fro,
      And that is best.

You know that of yours, your feeblest one
And dearest may live long years alone,
      Unloved unblest ;

Mine are cherished of saints around God's throne,
And that is best.

You must dread for yours the crime that sears,
Dark guilt unwashed by repentant tears,
And unconfessed;
Mine entered spotless on eternal years,
O, how much the best!

But grief is selfish; I cannot see
Always why I should so stricken be,
More than the rest;
But I know that, as well as for them, for me
God did the best!

MORNING-GLORY.

WONDROUS interlacement!
Holding fast to threads by green and silky rings,
With the dawn it spreads its white and purple wings;
Generous in its bloom, and sheltering while it clings,
Sturdy morning-glory.

Creeping through the casement,
Slanting to the floor in dusty, shining beams,
Dancing on the door in quick, fantastic gleams,

Comes the new day's light, and pours in tideless
          streams,
    Golden morning-glory.

In the lowly basement,
Rocking in the sun, the baby's cradle stands;
Now the little one thrusts out his rosy hands;
Soon his eyes will open; then in all the lands
    No such morning-glory!

OCTOBER.

ENDING above the spicy woods which
          blaze,
    Arch skies so blue they flash, and hold the
          sun
Immeasurably far; the waters run
Too slow, so freighted are the river-ways
With gold of elms and birches from the maze
Of forests. Chestnuts, clicking one by one,
Escape from satin burs; her fringes done,
The gentian spreads them out in sunny days,
And, like late revelers at dawn, the chance
Of one sweet, mad, last hour, all things assail,
And conquering, flush and spin; while, to enhance
The spell, by sunset door, wrapped in a veil
Of red and purple mists, the summer, pale,
Steals back alone for one more song and dance.

MY BEES.

AN ALLEGORY.

"BEES, sweet bees!" I said, "that nearest field
Is shining white with fragrant immortelles.
Fly swiftly there and drain those honey wells."
Then, spicy pines the sunny hive to shield,
I set, and patient for the autumn's yield
Of sweet I waited.   When the village bells
Rang frosty clear, and from their satin cells
The chestnuts leaped, rejoicing, I unsealed
My hive.   Alas! no snowy honey there
Was stored. My wicked bees had borne away
Their queen and left no trace.   That very day,
An idle drone who sauntered through the air
I tracked and followed, and he led me where
My truant bees and stolen honey lay.
Twice faithless bees! They had sought out to eat
Rank, bitter herbs. The honey was not sweet.

THE ABBOT PAPHNUTIUS.

NOW on the gray stone floor Paphnutius knelt
Scourging his breast, and drawing tight his
    belt
Of bloody nails.

                "O God, dear God!" he cried,
"These many years that I have crucified
My sinful flesh, and called upon thee night
And day, are they all reckoned in thy sight?
And wilt thou tell me now which saint of thine
I am most like? and is there bond or sign
That I can find him by and win him here,
That we may dwell as brothers close and dear?"

  Silent the river kept its gentle flow
Beneath the walls; the ash-trees to and fro
Swayed silent, save a sigh; a sunbeam laid
Its bar along the Abbot's beads, which made
Uncanny rhythm across the quiet air,
The only ghost of sound which sounded there,
As fast their smooth-worn balls he turned and told,
And trembled, thinking he had been too bold.
But suddenly, with solemn clang and swell,
In the high tower rang out the vesper-bell;
And subtly hidden in the pealing tones,
Melodious dropping from celestial thrones,
These words the glad Paphnutius thrilling heard:
"Be not afraid! In this thou hast not erred;

Of all my saints, the one whose heart most suits
To thine is one who, playing reedy flutes,
In the great market-place goes up and down,
While men and women dance, in yonder town."

    Oh, much Paphnutius wondered, as he went
To robe him for the journey. Day was spent,
And cunning night had spread and lit her snares
For souls made weak by weariness and cares,
When to the glittering town the Abbot came.
With secret shudder, half affright, half shame,
Close cowled, he mingled in the babbling throng,
And with reluctant feet was borne along
To where, by torches' fitful glare and smoke,
A band of wantons danced, and screamed, and spoke
Such words as fill pure men with shrinking fear.
" Good Lord deliver me ! Can he be here,"
The frightened Abbot said, " the man I seek?"
Lo, as he spoke, a man reeled dizzy, weak
With ribald laughter, clutching him by gown
And shoulder; and before his feet threw down
Soft twanging flutes, which rolled upon the stone
And broke. Outcried the Abbot with a groan,
Seizing the player firm in mighty hands,
" O man ! what doest thou with these vile bands
Of harlots ? God hath told to me thou art
A saint of his, and one whose life and heart
Are like my own ; and I have journeyed here
For naught but finding thee."

                              In maze and fear,
The player lifted up his blood-shot eyes,

And stammered drunkenly, " Good father, lies
Thy road some other way. Take better heed
Next time thou seekest saints ! One single deed
Of good I never did. I live in sins.
Unhand me now ! another dance begins."
" Flute-player," said the Abbot, stern and sweet,
" God cannot lie ! Some deed thou hast done meet
For serving him. Bethink thee now, and tell.
Where was it that the blessed chance befell ? "
Half-sobered by the Abbot's voice and mien,
The player spoke again, " No more I ween
Of serving God, than if no God there were ;
But now I do remember me of her
That once I saved from hands of robber-men,
Whose chief I was. I know I wondered then
What new blood could have quickened in my veins.
I gave her, spite myself, of our rich gains
Three hundred pieces of good gold, to free
Her husband and her sons from slavery.
But love of God had nought to do with this :
I know him, love him not ; I do not miss
Nor find him in the world. I love my sins.
Now let me go ! another dance begins."
" Yes, go ! " the Abbot gently said, and took
His grasp from off his arm. " But, brother, look,
If God has thus to thee this one good deed
So fully counted, wilt thou not take heed
Thyself, remembering him ? "

       Then homeward slow,
Alone and sad, where he had thought to go

Triumphant with a new-found brother-saint,
The Abbot went. But vain he set restraint
Upon his wondering thoughts : through prayer, through
    chant,
The question ever rang, " What could God want
To teach me, showing me that sinful man
As saint of nearest kin to me, who can
Abide no sin of thought or deed."

                                        Three days
The Abbot went his patient, silent ways.
The river lapped in gentle, silent flow
The cloister-wall; the ash-trees to and fro
Swayed silent, save a sigh : the third night, came —
Low rapping at the cloister-door, in shame
And fear — the player!

                         Then Paphnutius rose,
His pale face kindled red with joyful glows ;
The monks in angry, speechless wonder stood,
Seeing this vagabond to brotherhood
Made so soon welcome. But the Abbot said,
"O brothers! this flute-player in such stead
Is held of God, that, when in loneliness
I knelt and prayed for some new saint to bless
Our house, God spoke, and told me this man's name,
As his who should be brother when he came."

  Flute-player and Paphnutius both have slept
In dust for centuries. The world has kept
No record of them save this tale, which sets
But bootless lesson : still the world forgets

That God knows best what hearts are counted his;
Still men deny the thing whose sign they miss;
Still pious souls pray as Paphnutius prayed
For brother-souls in their own semblance made;
And slowly learn, with outcries and complaints,
That publicans and sinners may be saints!

NOON.

SWEET, delusive Noon,
    Which the morning climbs to find;
O moment sped too soon,
    And morning left behind;

While pale gray hours descend
    Fast on the farther slope,
Where a darkness marks the end
    Of that day's work and hope.

O Noon, if thou couldst stay!
    Were there but spell to arrest
Thy magic moment, — to slay
    Night on the fair sky's breast,

Or make the morning haste,
    Or the chilly evening tarry,
And the liquid light they waste
    Give thee, O Noon, to carry!

NOON.

O cruel, stinted drop,
  In sapphire chalice so deep
That if million suns should stop
  Its walls their light could keep!

   .   .   .   .   .

O Love, O Joys above
  All words of my telling, stay!
Does your swiftness mean that love
  Has day, and noon of day?

This sweetness more, more sweet,
  And this brightness growing bright,
This silent, delicious heat,
  This dearer, tenderer light,—

O Love, mean these a noon,
  A noon which thou climb'st to find,
That moment over too soon,
  With morning left behind?

O Love, we kneel, we pray,
  For our sweet Love's precious sake;
Set here the bound of our day;
  Grant us this choice we make.

We fear the gray hour's sight,
  The moment over too soon;
Spare us the chill of the night;
  We will forego our noon!

IN THE PASS.

ACROSS my road a mountain rose of rock, —
Fierce, naked rock. Its shadow, black and
    chill,
Shut out the sun. Gray clouds, which
    seemed to mock
With cruel challenges my helpless will,
Sprang up and scaled the steepest crags. The shrill
Winds, two and two, went breathless out and in,
Filling tne darkened air with evil din.

I turned away my weary steps and said :
"This must be confine of some fearful place ;
Here is no path for mortal man to tread.
Who enters here will tremble, face to face
With powers of darkness, whose unearthly race
In cloud and wind and storm delights to dwell,
Ruling them all.by an uncanny spell."

The guide but smiled, and, holding fast my hand,
Compelled me up a path I had not seen.
It wound round ledges where I scarce could stand ;
It plunged to sudden sunless depths between
Immeasurable cliffs, which seemed to lean
Together, closing as we passed, like door
Of dungeon which would open nevermore.

I said again: " I will not go. This way
Is not for mortal feet." Again the guide

But smiled, and I again could but obey.
The path grew narrow; thundering by its side,
As loud as ocean at its highest tide,
A river rushed, all black, and green, and white,
A boiling stream of molten malachite.

Sudden I heard a joyous cry, " Behold, behold !"
And, smiling still on me, the good guide turned,
And pointed where broad, sunny fields unrolled
And spread like banners; green, so green it burned,
And lit the air like red; and blue which yearned
From all the lofty dome of sky, and bent
And folded low and circling like a tent;

And forests ranged like armies, round and round,
At feet of mountains of eternal snow;
And valleys all alive with happy sound;
The song of birds; swift brooks' delicious flow;
The mystic hum of million things that grow;
The stir of men; and gladdening every way,
Voices of little children at their play;

And shining banks of flowers which words refuse
To paint; such colors as in summer light
The rarest, fleetest summer rainbows use,
But set in gold of sun, and silver white
Of dew, as thick as gems which blind the sight
On altar fronts, inlaid with priceless things,
The jewelled gifts of centuries of kings.

Then, sitting half in dream, and half in fear
Of how such wondrous miracle were wrought.

Thy name, dear friend, I sudden seemed to hear
Through all the charmed air.
                         My loving thought
Through patient years had vainly groped and sought,
And found no hidden thing so rare, so good,
That it might furnish thy similitude.

O noble soul, whose strengths like mountains stand,
Whose purposes, like adamantine stone,
Bar roads to feeble feet, and wrap the land
In seeming shadow, thou, too, hast thine own
Sweet valleys full of flowers, for me alone,
Unseen, unknown, undreamed of by the mass,
Who do not know the secret of the Pass.

CORTINA D'AMPEZZO, AMPEZZO PASS, June 22, 1869.

AMREETA WINE.

HE rose up from the golden feast,
    And her voice rang like the sea ;
" Sir Knight, put down thy glass and come
    To the battlement with me.

" That was a charmed wine thou drank'st,
   Signed white from heaven, signed black from hell.
Alas ! alas ! for the bitter thing
   The sign hath forced thy lips to tell ! "

"Ho here!   Ho there!   Lift up and bear
    My choice wine out," she said;
"That which hath brand of a clasping hand,
    And the seal blood-red."

"Ho here!   Ho there!   To the castle stair
    Bear all that branded wine ;
And dash it far, where the breakers are
    Whitest, of the brine !

"Let no man dare to shrink or spare,
    Or one red drop to spill ;
Of the endless pain of that wine's hot stain
    Let the salt sea bear its fill.

"O woe of mine! O woe of thine !
    O woe of endless thirst !
O woe for the Amreeta wine,
    By fate and thee accurst !"

The knight spake words of sore dismay
    But her face was white like stone ;
She saw him mount and ride away,
    And made no moan.

The wind blew east, the wind blew west,
    The airs from sepulchres ;
No royal heart in all of them
    So dead as hers!

SOLITUDE.

"SOLITUDE," I said, "sweet Solitude!
I follow fast; I kneel to find thy trace;
I listen low in every secret place;
I lay rough hand on eager human lips;
I set aside all near companionships;
I know thou hast a subtler, rarer good.
O Priestess, how shalt thou be found and wooed?"
I tracked her where she passed in trackless fields;
I trod her path where footprint had not staid
In sunless woods; I stopped to hark where laid
Her very shadow its great bound of light
And gloom in lifeless arctic day and night;
And where, to tropic sun, mid-ocean yields
Its silent, windless waves, like mirror-shields;

But found her not. Great tribes roamed free
In every trackless field and wood. More plain
Than speech I heard their voice: in rain, the rain
Of endless chatter, and in sun, the sun
Of merry laughing noise, were never done.
All silence dinned with sound; and, jostling me,
In every place, went crowds I could not see.

In anger, then, at last I cried, "Betray
Whomever thou canst cheat, O Solitude,
With promise of thy subtler, rarer good!

I seek my joy henceforth in haunts of men,
Forgetting thee, where thou hast never been!"
When, lo! that instant sounded close and sweet,
Above the rushing of the city street,
The voice of Solitude herself, to say,
"Ha, loving comrade, met at last! Which way?"

"NOT AS I WILL."

BLINDFOLDED and alone I stand
  With unknown thresholds on each hand;
  The darkness deepens as I grope,
  Afraid to fear, afraid to hope:
Yet this one thing I learn to know
Each day more surely as I go,
That doors are opened, ways are made,
Burdens are lifted or are laid,
By some great law unseen and still,
Unfathomed purpose to fulfil,
    "Not as I will."

Blindfolded and alone I wait;
Loss seems too bitter, gain too late;
Too heavy burdens in the load
And too few helpers on the road;
And joy is weak and grief is strong,
And years and days so long, so long:
Yet this one thing I learn to know
Each day more surely as I go,

That I am glad the good and ill
By changeless law are ordered still,
    "Not as I will."

"Not as I will": the sound grows sweet
Each time my lips the words repeat.
"Not as I will": the darkness feels
More safe than light when this thought steals
Like whispered voice to calm and bless
All unrest and all loneliness.
"Not as I will," because the One
Who loved us first and best has gone
Before us on the road, and still
For us must all his love fulfil,
    "Not as we will."

LAND.

LAND, sweet land! New World! my
  world!
No mortal knows what seas I sail
  With hope and faith which never fail,
With heart and will which never quail,
Till on thy shore my sails are furled,
O land, sweet land! New World! my world!

O land, sweet land! New World! my world!
I cross again, again, again
The magic seas. Each time I reign
Crowned conqueror. Each time remain
New shores on which my sails are furled,
A sweeter land! A newer world!

O world, New World! Sweet land, my land!
I come to-day, as first I came.
The sea is swift, the sky is flame.
My low song sings thy nameless name.
Lovers who love, ye understand!
O sweetest world! O sweetest land!

OCTOBER 2d, 1871.

OPPORTUNITY.

I DO not know if, climbing some steep hill
Through fragrant wooded pass, this glimpse
    I bought ;
Or whether in some midday I was caught
To upper air, where visions of God's will
In pictures to our quickened sense fulfil
His word.　But this I saw :
                  A path I sought
Through wall of rock.　No human fingers wrought
The golden gates which opened, sudden, still,
And wide.　My fear was hushed by my delight.
Surpassing fair the lands ; my path lay plain ;
Alas ! so spell-bound, feasting on the sight,
I paused, that I but reached the threshold bright,
When, swinging swift, the golden gates again
Were rocky walls, by which I wept in vain !

WHEN THE BABY DIED.

I.

WHEN the baby died,
    On every side
White lilies and blue violets were strown ;
Unreasoning, the mother's heart made moan:

"Who counted all these flowers which have grown
    Unhindered in their bloom?
  Was there not room,
O Earth, and God, couldst thou not care
For mine a little longer? Fare
Thy way, O Earth! All life, all death
For me ceased with my baby's breath;
All Heaven I forget or doubt.
    Within, without,
Is idle chance, more pitiless than law."
And that was all the mother saw.

        II.

    When the baby died,
    On every side
Rose strangers' voices, hard and harsh and loud.
The baby was not wrapped in any shroud.
The mother made no sound. Her head was bowed
That men's eyes might not see
    Her misery;
But in her bitter heart she said,
"Ah me! 't is well that he is dead,
My boy for whom there was no food.
If there were God, and God were good,
All human hearts at least might keep
    The right to weep
Their dead. There is no God, but cruel law."
And that was all the mother saw.

III.

When the baby died,
On every side
Swift angels came in shining, singing bands,
And bore the little one, with gentle hands,
Into the sunshine of the spirit lands.
      And Christ the Shepherd said,
    " Let them be led
In gardens nearest to the earth.
One mother weepeth over birth,
Another weepeth over death ;
In vain all Heaven answereth.
Laughs from the little ones may reach
      Their ears, and teach
Them what, so blind with tears, they never saw, —
That of all life, all death, God's love is law."

"OLD LAMPS FOR NEW."

SOUL! wert thou a poor maid-servant, weak
And foolish, and unknowing how the walls
Of shining stones and silver, and fine gold,
Which made our dwelling glorious, our life
Assured, were built, that thou must spring at call
Of our most deadly foe, lured by the sound

And glitter of his hollow brass, and give
Into his treacherous hands our all ?
                                And now
For thee and me remaineth nothing more,
But cold and hunger and the desert !
                                Soul,
Rise up and follow him, and tarry not,
Nor dare to call thy life thine own, until
Thou hast waylaid him sitting at his feast,
And torn our talisman from off his breast !

FEAST.

FOR days when guests unbidden
    Walk in my sun,
With steps that roam unchidden,
    And overrun
My vines and flowers, and hands
That rob on all my lands, —
For such days, still there stands
    One banquet, one !

One banquet which, spread under
    A magic mist,
I taste, until they wonder
    What light has kissed
My eyes, and where the grapes
Have hung, whose red escapes
In mounting, mantling shapes,
    And heats my wrist.

Crowned with its rosy flowers,
    Pouring its wine,
Glide faithful ghosts of hours
    Long dead: no sign
They show of death, or chill,
But glowing, smiling still,
Love's utmost joy fulfil
    At word of mine.

And ringeth through my garden,
    The tireless pace
Of silver-mailed warden,
    With eastward face,
Who calmly bides the night,
And in each first, red light,
Reads prophecy aright
    Of that day's grace,

When guests that are unbidden
    Shall all have ceased;
And thy dear arms unchidden,
    My love, my priest,
Shall hold me while the hours
That were, and are, fling flowers,
And Hope, the warden, pours
    Wine for our feast.

TWO SUNDAYS.

I.

BABY, alone, in a lowly door,
Which climbing woodbine made still lower,
Sat playing with lilies in the sun.
The loud church-bells had just begun ;
The kitten pounced in the sparkling grass
At stealthy spiders that tried to pass ;
The big watch-dog kept a threatening eye
On me, as I lingered, walking by.

The lilies grew high, and she reached up
On tiny tiptoes to each gold cup ;
And laughed aloud, and talked, and clapped
Her small, brown hands, as the tough stems snapped.
And flowers fell till the broad hearthstone
Was covered, and only the topmost one
Of the lilies left.   In sobered glee
She said to herself, " That's older than me ! "

II.

Two strong men through the lowly door,
With uneven steps, the baby bore ;
They had set the bier on the lily bed ;
The lily she left was crushed and dead.
The slow, sad bells had just begun,

The kitten crouched, afraid, in the sun ;
And the poor watch-dog, in bewildered pain,
Took no notice of me as I joined the train.

SHOWBREAD.

PAST imaged pillars, wrought of fir and palm,
　　Past bright pomegranates, swinging on their
　　　　chain,
　　And bars of Tyrian cedar, overlain
With gold, and past the molten sea whose calm
Waves drink the offerings of spice and balm,
Lit by the seven sacred lamps whose rain
Of fragrant fire the almond bowls detain,
Past clear-eyed cherubim, without alarm,
And into shadow of the mercy-seat
We pressed.　　　No priest with onyx-stones to meet
Us there !　Alone our hunger, face to face
With God, ate of the showbread, sacred, sweet ;
And listening, heard these words of heavenly grace,—
"One greater than the temple fills this place.'

TIDES.

PATIENT shore, that canst not go to meet
Thy love, the restless sea, how comfortest
Thou all thy loneliness? Art thou at rest,
When, loosing his strong arms from round
    thy feet,
He turns away? Know'st thou, however sweet
That other shore may be, that to thy breast
He must return? And when in sterner test
He folds thee to a heart which does not beat,
Wraps thee in ice, and gives no smile, no kiss,
To break long wintry days, still dost thou miss
Naught from thy trust? Still wait, unfaltering,
The higher, warmer waves which leap in spring?
O sweet, wise shore, to be so satisfied!
O heart, learn from the shore! Love has a tide!

TRIBUTE.

R. W. E.

MIDWAY in summer, face to face, a king
I met. No king so gentle and so wise.
He calls no man his subject; but his eyes,
    In midst of benediction, questioning,
Each soul compel. A first-fruits offering

Each soul must owe to him whose fair land lies
Wherever God has his. No white dove flies
Too white, no wine too red and rich, to bring.
With sudden penitence for all her waste,
My soul to yield her scanty hoards made haste,
When lo! they shrank and failed me in that need,
Like wizard's gold, by worthless dust replaced.
My speechless grief, the king, with tender heed,
Thus soothed: "These ashes sow. They are true seed."
O king! in other summer may I stand
Before thee yet, the full ear in my hand!

"ALMS AT THE BEAUTIFUL GATE."

AH, how shall we, lame from the mother's womb,
The temple enter! Beautiful in vain
For us, the gate, where we, in double pain,
Of suffering and of loss, can find no room;
Whose whiteness only makes our outer gloom
The blacker, and whose shining steps, more plain
Than words, mock cripples weeping to attain
The inner courts, where censers, sweet perfume,
And music fill the air!
                    O sinful fear!
Dare not to doubt. Our helplessness laid near
That gate, is safe; our faith without alarms
Can wait; the good apostles will appear;

Our crippled beggary, made rich by alms
Of God, shall leap and praise, in grateful psalms.

CORONATION.

AT the king's gate the subtle noon
    Wove filmy yellow nets of sun;
    Into the drowsy snare too soon
    The guards fell one by one.

Through the king's gate, unquestioned then,
    A beggar went, and laughed, "This brings
Me chance, at last, to see if men
    Fare better, being kings."

The king sat bowed beneath his crown,
    Propping his face with listless hand;
Watching the hour-glass sifting down
    Too slow its shining sand.

"Poor man, what wouldst thou have of me?"
    The beggar turned, and, pitying,
Replied, like one in dream, "Of thee,
    Nothing. I want the king."

Uprose the king, and from his head
    Shook off the crown and threw it by.
"O man, thou must have known," he said,
    "A greater king than I."

Through all the gates, unquestioned then,
  Went king and beggar hand in hand.
Whispered the king, " Shall I know when
  Before *his* throne I stand ? "

The beggar laughed. Free winds in haste
  Were wiping from the king's hot brow
The crimson lines the crown had traced.
  " This is his presence now."

At the kings's gate, the crafty noon
  Unwove its yellow nets of sun ;
Out of their sleep in terror soon
  The guards waked one by one.

" Ho here ! Ho there ! Has no man seen
  The king ? " The cry ran to and fro ;
Beggar and king, they laughed, I ween,
  . The laugh that free men know.

On the king's gate the moss grew gray ;
  The king came not. They called him dead ;
And made his eldest son one day
  Slave in his father's stead.

MY NEW FRIEND

SHALLOW voice said, bitterly, "New
    friend!"
As if the old alone were true, and, born
Of sudden freak, the new deserved but
    scorn
And deep distrust.
              If love could condescend,
What scorn in turn! Do men old garments mend
With new? And put the new wine, red at morn,
Into the last year's bottles, thin and worn?
But love and loving need not to defend
Themselves. The new is older than the old;
And newest friend is oldest friend in this,
That, waiting him, we longest grieved to miss
One thing we sought.
              I think when we behold
Full Heaven, we say not, "Why was this not told?"
But, "Ah! For years we've waited for this bliss!"

ASTERS AND GOLDEN ROD.

I KNOW the lands are lit
With all the autumn blaze of Golden Rod;
And everywhere the Purple Asters nod
And bend and wave and flit.

But when the names I hear,
I never picture how their pageant lies
Spread out in tender stateliness of guise,
　The fairest of the year.

I only see one nook,
A wooded nook — half sun, half shade —
Where one I love his footsteps sudden stayed,
And whispered, " Darling, look!"

Two oak leaves, vivid green,
Hung low among the ferns, and parted wide;
While purple Aster Stars, close side by side,
Like faces peered between.

Like maiden faces set
In vine-wreathed window, waiting shy and glad
For joys whose dim, mysterious promise had
But promise been, as yet.

And, like proud lovers bent,
In regal courtesy, as kings might woo,
Tall Golden Rods, bareheaded in the dew,
Above the Asters leant.

    Ah, me!   Lands will be lit
With every autumn's blaze of Golden Rod,
And purple Asters everywhere will nod
    And bend and wave and flit;

    Until, like ripened seed,
This little earth itself, some noon, shall float
Off into space, a tiny shining mote,
    Which none but God will heed;

    But never more will be
Sweet Asters peering through that branch of oak
To hear such precious words as dear lips spoke
    That sunny day to me.

TWO LOVES.

LOVE beckoned me to come more near,
    And wait, two women's songs to hear:
    The songs ran sweet, the songs ran clear;
        It seemed they never could be done.
One woman sat and sang in shade,
    Her still hands on her bosom laid;
        The other sat and sang in sun.

"I love my love," the one song said,
"Because he lifts such kingly head,
And walks with such a kingly tread,

That men kneel down, and men confess;
And women, in soft, sad surprise,
Acknowledge, by their longing eyes,
   His beauty and his goodliness.

"His glory is my soul's estate;
Breathless with love I watch and wait
The hours of his triumphant fate,
   Knowing that far the greater part
Of all his joy in all his fame
Surrenders to my whispered name
   In secret places of his heart.

"And oh! I love my love again
With love incredulous of pain,
Because I know my beauty's chain
   Binds him so sure, binds him so fast.
I know there is not one swift bliss
Which men may know, that he can miss,
   Or say of it that it is past."

This was her song, who sat in sun;
It seemed it never would be done,
Unless its joy should all outrun
   Slow speech, and fall of its own weight;
As fountains their sweet source recall,
And, pausing sudden, break and fall,
   In murmur inarticulate.

The other song, more soft, more low,
Out of the shade came floating slow,
As autumn leaves swim to and fro

In golden seas of sunny air.
Her meek hands on her bosom laid,
Sign of the cross unwitting made;
   The woman was not young nor fair.

"I love my love," the low song said,
Because his noble, kingly head
Is bowed, while, with most patient tread,
   He walks hard paths he did not choose,
Smiling where other men would grieve,
Heart-glad if other men receive
   Their fill of joys which he must lose.

"I see each failure he must make,
Each step he cannot but mistake;
And, weeping for his soul's dear sake,
   I set my faith with love's own seal,—
Token of all which he might be,
Token of all he is to me,
   As God and my own heart reveal.

"And oh! I love my love again,
With love which is as strong as pain,
Because I know that by the chain
   Of beauty's bond I cannot bind;
The sweetest things which make men's bliss,
In loving me, my love must miss,
   In loving me, he cannot find.

"So, fearing lest I may not feed
Always his utmost want and need,
In trust for her who can succeed

Where I must fail, his love's estate
I solemn hold. Its rightful heir,
A woman younger and more fair,
  Loving my love, I bide and wait."

This was her song, who sat in shade,
Her meek hands on her bosom laid,
Sign of the cross unwitting made;
  She was not young, she was not fair:
The sad notes floated sweet and slow,
As autumn leaves swim to and fro
  On golden seas of sunny air.

"O Love!" I said, "which loveth best?
O Love, dear Love! which wins thy rest?"
But Love was gone; and, in the west,
  The sun, which gave one woman sun,
And gave the other woman shade,
Sank down; on each the cold night laid
  Its silence, and each song was done.

THE GOOD SHEPHERD.

LATE at night I saw the shepherd
   Toiling slow along the hill,
   With a smile of joy and patience,
      Facing night winds strong and chill.
In his arms and in his bosom
   Lay the lambs content and still.

When the day broke, from the valley
   I looked up and saw no more
Of the patient, smiling shepherd
   I had seen the night before ;
But new mounds along the hillside
   Lay in sunshine, frozen hoar !

LOVE'S FULFILLING.

LOVE is weak
Which counts the answers and the
  gains,
Weighs all the losses and the pains,
And eagerly each fond word drains
  A joy to seek.

When Love is strong,
It never tarries to take heed,
Or know if its return exceed
Its gift; in its sweet haste no greed,
  No strifes belong.

It hardly asks
If it be loved at all; to take
So barren seems, when it can make
Such bliss, for the beloved sake,
  Of bitter tasks.

Its ecstasy
Could find hard death so beauteous,
It sees through tears how Christ loved us,
And speaks, in saying "I love thus,"
  No blasphemy.

So much we miss
If love is weak, so much we gain

If love is strong, God thinks no pain
Too sharp or lasting to ordain
To teach us this.

WOOED.

I.

ITH voice all confident, I knelt and cried,
"Behold me at thy feet, O darling queen!
I kiss, round lowest hem, thy robe of
green;
In all thy temples I have prophesied,
And cast out devils in thy name. Confide
In me. Lift up the veil that hangs between
My eyes and thy dear face. Tell me what mean
The voices of thy people." Far and wide
The lovely queen's sweet kingdoms lie. I found
My way to follow her to utmost bound
Of all; and listened, listened, nights and days,
To every smallest sound on her highways;
But could not once her golden sceptre reach,
Nor win the secret of her people's speech.

WON.

II.

WEARIED at last, and sad, I cried, "Refuse
    Me what thou wilt, my queen! At thy
       dear feet
    Henceforth I lie and sleep, and dream, and
       eat
Thy locusts and wild honey. Thou mayst choose,
Perhaps, that I the latchet of thy shoes
One day unfasten. Ever incomplete
Leave my desire, too bold, to see thy sweet,
Unveiled face; to know what words they use
Who serve around thy throne."
                              Lo! as I lay,
In such surrender, on that summer day,
And sought not, stirred not, came the radiant queen,
Sweeping me with her robe of leafy green,
And kissed me everywhere that kiss could go;
While all her royal train I longed to know,
The swallow leading, crowded up to teach
Me all the secrets of their song and speech.

ARIADNE'S FAREWELL.

HE daughter of a king, how should I know
That there were tinsels wearing face of gold,
And worthless glass, which in the sunlight's
    hold
Could shameless answer back my diamond's glow
With cheat of kindred fire ? The currents slow,
And deep, and strong, and stainless, which had rolled
Through royal veins for ages, what had told
To them, that hasty heat and lie could show
As quick and warm a red as theirs ?
                                    Go free !
The sun is breaking on the sea's blue shield
Its golden lances; by their gleam I see
Thy ship's white sails. Go free, if scorn can yield
Thee freedom !
            Then, alone, my love and I, —
We both are royal; we know how to die.

THOUGHT.

MESSENGER, art thou the king, or I ?
Thou dalliest outside the palace gate
Till on thine idle armor lie the late
And heavy dews: the morn's bright, scorn-
    ful eye
Reminds thee ; then, in subtle mockery,

Thou smilest at the window where I wait,
Who bade thee ride for life. In empty state
My days go on, while false hours prophesy
Thy quick return ; at last, in sad despair,
I cease to bid thee, leave thee free as air ;
When lo, thou stand'st before me glad and fleet,
And lay'st undreamed-of treasures at my feet.
Ah ! messenger, thy royal blood to buy,
I am too poor. Thou art the king, not I.

MORDECAI.

MAKE friends with him ! He is of royal line,
Although he sits in rags. Not all of thine
Array of splendor, pomp of high estate,
Can buy him from his place within the gate,
The king's gate of thy happiness, where he,
Yes, even he, the Jew, remaineth free,
Never obeisance making, never scorn
Betraying of thy silver and new-born
Delight. Make friends with him, for unawares
The charmèd secret of thy joys he bears ;
Be glad, so long as his black sackcloth, late
And early, thwarts thy sun ; for if in hate
Thou plottest for his blood, thy own death-cry,
Not his, comes from the gallows, cubits high.

LOCUSTS AND WILD HONEY.

HOSPITABLE wilderness,
  I know thy secret sign;
All human welcome seemeth less
  To me than thine.

Such messengers to show me where
  Is water for my feet;
Such perfume poured upon my hair,
  Costly and sweet.

Such couch, such canopy, such floor,
  Such royal banquet spread;
Such music through the open door,
  So little said.

So much bestowed and understood,
  Such flavored courtesy,
And only kings of unmixed blood
  For company.

Such rhythmic tales of ancient lores,
  Of sweet and hidden things,
Rehearsed by sacred troubadours
  On tireless wings.

Such secrets of dominion set
  Unstinted for my choice,

Such mysteries, unuttered yet,
    Waiting a voice.

O hospitable wilderness,
    For thee I long and pine;
All human welcome seemeth less
    To me than thine.

A MOTHER'S FAREWELL TO A VOYAGER.

"—— sends love and good-by. She thinks she sees the four quarters of the globe when she looks into the faces of her four children. November 2, 1868."

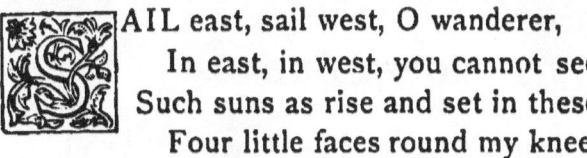

SAIL east, sail west, O wanderer,
    In east, in west, you cannot see
Such suns as rise and set in these
    Four little faces round my knee.

Blue as the north my first-born's eyes;
    Her yellow hair hides brow of snow;
Like conquerors from the North she brought
    The sweet subjection mothers know.

Glad and sad, and changed in an hour,
    My next girl's face is tropic sea,
Where laden winds, whose secret none
    Can tell, sweep on unceasingly.

Grave and searching, with hidden fire,
  My black-eyed boy kneels like a priest;
I know that, looking where he looks,
  We shall see the "Star in the East."

No name as yet my baby has,
  Her rosy hands are just uncurled;
But with wet eyes we kiss her cheeks,
  And thank God for our sweet "new world."

Sail east, sail west, dear wanderer!
  God cares for you and cares for me;
He knows for which of us 't was best
  To stay with children round her knee.

STEAMSHIP CHINA, November 12, 1868.

"DROPPED DEAD."

LL royal strengths in life, until the end,
  Will bear themselves still royally. Degrees
Of dying they know not: the muddy lees
  They will not drink: no man shall see
      them bend
Or slacken in the storm: no man can lend
To them. Those feeble souls who crouch on knees
That fail, and cling to shadows of lost ease,
Death tortures. But, as kings to kings may send,
He challenges the strong.
              Such death as this

O'ertakes great love ; a lesser love will miss
Such stroke ; may dwindle painfully away,
And fade, and simply cease to breathe, some day.
But great loves, to the last, have pulses red ;
All great loves that have ever died dropped dead.

PRESENCE.

NAMELESS thing! which art and art not;
    spell
Whose bond can bind the powers of the air,
Compelling them thy face to hide or bear.
O voice ! which, bringing not the faintest swell
Of sound, canst in the air so crowd and dwell
That all sounds die. O sight! which needst no share
Of sun, which sav'st blind eyes from their despair,
O touch ! which dost not touch, and yet canst tell
To waiting flesh, by thy caress complete,
The whole of love, till veins grow red with heat ;
O life of life ! to which graves are not girt
With terror, and all death can bring no hurt.
O mystery of blessing ! never lift
Thy veil ! our one inalienable gift !

POLAR DAYS.

As some poor piteous Lapp., who under firs
Which bend and break with load of arctic
    snows
    Has crept and crouched to watch when
        crimson glows
Begin, feels in his veins the thrilling stirs
Of warmer life, e'en while his fear deters
His trust; and when the orange turns to rose
In vain, and widening to the westward goes
The ruddy beam and fades, heartsick defers
His hope, and shivers through one more long night
Of sunless day; —
            So watching, one by one,
The faintest glimmers of the morn's gray light,
The sleepless exiled heart waits for the bright
Full day, and hopes till all its hours are done,
That the next one will bring its love, its sun.

TRUTH.

TRUTH, art thou relentless? Wilt thou
    rest
Never? From solitude to solitude
    Eternally wilt thou escape? Thy good
And beauty luring us to fatal quest,
Foredoomed to endless loss?

                        O royal guest
Of Nature's centuries, no spot so rude,
So void, thy secret cannot there elude
Our grasp ; no thing too subtle to attest
Her royal sheltering ; from spheres to spheres
Of light, through the incalculable years ;
From force to force, through rock, through sound,
        through flame,
Our worship wrests but echo of thy name,
And builds at last, with patient stone, and sod,
And tears, its altar " to the unknown God."

HER EYES.

THAT they are brown, no man will dare to
        say
He knows. And yet I think that no man's
        look
Ever those depths of light and shade forsook,
Until their gentle pain warned him away.
Of all sweet things I know but one which may
Be likened to her eyes.
                        When, in deep nook
Of some green field, the water of a brook
Makes lingering, whirling eddy in its way,
Round soft drowned leaves ; and in a flash of sun
They turn to gold, until the ripples run

Now brown, now yellow, changing as by some
Swift spell.
        I know not with what body come
The saints. But this I know, my Paradise
Will mean the resurrection of her eyes.

THE WALL-FLOWER OF THE RUINS OF ROME.

GOLDEN-WINGED, on guard at crumbled gate
And fallen wall of emperors and kings,
Whose very names are now forgotten things,
Thou standest here, in faithfulness to wait
The centuries through, and of the ancient state
Keep up the semblance. Never footstep rings
Across the stones ; and yet, if sun but flings
One ray, a gleam, like gleam of burnished plate
On mailed men, thy hands have lit, and sent
Along the gray and tottering battlement,
And flung out yellow banners, pricked with red,
Which need not shame a royal house to spread.
Ah, golden-winged, the whole of thy deep spell
I cannot fathom, and thou wilt not tell.

SHADOWS OF BIRDS.

IN darkened air, alone with pain,
I lay. Like links of heavy chain
The minutes sounded, measuring day,
And slipping lifelessly away.
Sudden across my silent room
A shadow darker than its gloom
Swept swift; a shadow slim and small
Which poised and darted on the wall,
And vanished quickly as it came;
A shadow, yet it lit like flame;
A shadow, yet I heard it sing,
And heard the rustle of its wing,
Till every pulse with joy was stirred;
It was the shadow of a bird!

Only the shadow! Yet it made
Full summer everywhere it strayed;
And every bird I ever knew
Back and forth in the summer flew;
And breezes wafted over me
The scent of every flower and tree;
Till I forgot the pain and gloom
And silence of my darkened room.
Now, in the glorious open air,
I watch the birds fly here and there;

And wonder, as each swift wing cleaves
The sky, if some poor soul that grieves
In lonely, darkened, silent walls
Will catch the shadow as it falls!

GLIMPSES.

AS when on some great mountain-peak we stand,
  In breathless awe beneath its dome of sky,
  Whose multiplied horizons seem to lie
Beyond the bounds of earthly sea and land,
We find the circled space too vast, too grand,
And soothe our thoughts with restful memory
Of sudden sunlit glimpses we passed by
Too quickly, in our feverish demand
To reach the height, —
                    So, darling, when the brink
Of highest heaven we reach at last, I think
Even that great gladness will grow yet more glad,
As we, with eyes that are no longer sad,
Look back, while Life's horizons slowly sink,
To some swift moments which on earth we had.

TO A. C. L. B.

THY house hath gracious freedom, like the air
    Of open fields; its silence hath a speech
    Of royal welcome to the friends who reach
Its threshold, and its upper chambers bear,
Above their doors such spells, that, entering there
And laying off the dusty garments, each
Soul whispers to herself: "'T were like a breach
Of reverence in a temple could I dare
Here speak untruth, here wrong my inmost thought.
Here I grow strong and pure; here I may yield,
Without shamefacedness, the little brought
From out my poorer life, and stand revealed,
And glad, and trusting, in the sweet and rare
And tender presence which hath filled this air."

SNOW-DROPS IN ITALY.

LOYAL vestals in this land of sun,
    Your white cheeks flush not, and your virgin eyes
    Vouchsafe no lifted look. In vain the skies
Are red and pale with passion; swift clouds run
And beckon; warm winds call; long days are done
And nights are spent, and still by no surprise,
No lure can ye be tempted!

O, where lies
The spell by which your gentleness can shun
These heats? Is it your hidden zone of gold?
Or in the emerald whose glimmers show,
Scarce show, beneath your white robes' inner fold?
Vain question! Still your calm bright peace ye hold;
And yet ye set my pulses all aglow
With loyalty like yours to lands of snow.

DISTANCE.

SUBTILE secret of the air,
Making the things that are not, fair
Beyond the things that we can reach
And name with names of clumsy speech;
By shadow-worlds of purple haze
The sunniest of sunny days
Outweighing in our hearts' delight;
Opening the eyes of blinded sight;
Holding an echo in such hold,
Bidding a hope such wings unfold,
That present sounds and sights between
Can come and go, unheard, unseen, —
O subtile secret of the air,
Heaven itself is heavenly fair
By help of thee! The saints' good days
Are good, because the good Lord lays
No bound of shore along the sea
Of beautiful Eternity.

WHEN THE KINGS COME.

WHEN the Kings come to royal hunting seats
To find the royal joys of summer days,
The servants on the lofty watch-tower raise
A banner, whose swift token warning greets
The country. Threatening stern, an armed man meets
Each stranger, who, by pleasant forest-ways,
All unawares, has rambled till he strays
Too close to paths where, in the noonday heats,
The King, uncrowned, lies down to sleep. Such law
As this the human soul sets heart and face
And hand, when once its King has come. In awe,
And gladness too, all men behold what grace
Such royal presence to the eye can bring,
And how the heart and hand can guard their King.

COMING ACROSS.

EVERY sail is full set, and the sky
    And the sea blaze with light,
And the moon mid her virgins glides on
    As St. Ursula might;
And the throb of the pulse never stops,
    In the heart of the ship,

As her measures of water and fire
  She drinks down at a sip.
Yet I never can think, as I lie,
  And so wearily toss,
That by saint, or by star, or by ship,
  I am coming across;

But by light which I know in dear eyes
  That are bent on the sea,
And the touch I remember of hands
  That are waiting for me.
By the light of the eyes I could come,
  If the stars should all fail;
And I think, if the ship should go down,
  That the hands would prevail.
Ah! my darlings, you never will know
  How I pined in the loss
Of you all, and how breathless and glad
  I am coming across.

  STEAMSHIP RUSSIA, January 22, 1870.

THE TEACHER.

THE people listened, with short, indrawn
    breath,
  And eyes that were too steady set for tears.
  This one man's speech rolled off great loads
    of fears
From every heart, as sunlight scattereth

The clouds; hard doubts, which had been born of
    death,
Shone out as rain-drops shine when rainbow clears
The air. " O teacher," then I said, " thy years,
Are they not joy? Each word that issueth
From out thy lips, doth it return to bless
Thy own heart many fold?"
                      With weariness
Of tone he answered, and almost with scorn,
" I am, of all, most lone in loneliness;
I starve with hunger treading out their corn;
I die of travail while their souls are born."

DECORATION DAY.

I.

THE Eastern wizards do a wondrous thing,
   Which travellers, having seen, scarce dare
      to tell:
Dropping a seed in earth, by subtle spell
Of hidden heat they force the germ to spring
To instant life and growth; no faltering
'Twixt leaf and flower and fruit; they rise and swell
To perfect shape and size, as if there fell
Upon them all which seasons hold and bring.
But Love far greater magic shows to-day:
Lifting its feeble hands, which can but reach

The hands-breadth up, it stretches all the way
From earth to heaven, and, triumphant, each
Sweet wilting blossom sets, before it dies,
Full in the sight of smiling angels' eyes.

II.

But, ah ! the graves which no man names or knows ;
Uncounted graves, which never can be found ;
Graves of the precious " missing," where no sound
Of tender weeping will be heard, where goes
No loving step of kindred. O, how flows
And yearns our thought to them !   More holy ground
Of graves than this, we say, is that whose bound
Is secret till eternity disclose
Its sign.   But Nature knows her wilderness ;
There are no " missing " in her numbered ways.
In her great heart is no forgetfulness.
Each grave she keeps she will adorn, caress.
We cannot lay such wreaths as Summer lays,
And all her days are Decoration Days !

A THIRTEENTH-CENTURY PARABLE.

WHEN good Saint Louis reigned in France as
    king,
And William, Bishop of Paris, ministering
    To all the churches, kept them pure and glad,
There came one day a learned man, who had
Journeyed from distant provinces to find
His Bishop and unload his burdened mind.
Entering the Bishop's presence, he began
To speak: but sobs choked all his voice; tears ran
Like rain from out his eyes, and no words came
To tell his grief. Then said the Bishop:
                                "Shame
Not thyself so deeply, Master: no man
So sins but that the gracious Jesus can
Forgive an hundred thousand fold more guilt
Than his, and cleanse it by his dear blood spilt."
"I tell you, Sire," the Master said, "I must
Forever weep: I am accursed. I trust
Not in the holy altar-sacrament,
As taught to us; I cannot but dissent
From all the Church doth say of it: and yet
I know my doubts are but temptations set
By Satan's self, to sink my soul to hell.
O Sire, I am a wretched Infidel."
Then said the gentle Bishop:
                           "This one thing
Tell me, O honest Master, do they bring

Thee pleasure, these dark doubts?"
"O, no! my Sire,"
The weeping Master said: "they burn like fire
Within my bones."
"And could thy lips to speak
Thy doubts be bought by gold? And would'st thou
   seek
To shake a brother's faith?"
"I, Sire!" exclaimed
The Master. "I! I would be bruised and maimed,
And torn from limb to limb, ere I would say
Such words."
Then said the Bishop, smiling: "Lay
Aside now for a space thy grief and fear,
And listen. Soon my meaning will appear,
Though it be strangely hid at first below
My words.
Thou know'st that war is raging now
Between the King of England and of France;
Thou know'st that of our castles greatest chance
Of loss has La Rochelle, there in Poitou,
Lying so near the border. If to you
The King had given La Rochelle to hold,
And unto me — no less true man and bold,
Perhaps — the Castle of Laon to keep,
Far in the heart of France, where I might sleep
All day, all night, unharmed, if so I chose, —
So safe beyond the reach of all our foes
Lies Laon, — when the war is ended, who
Ought from the King to have the most thanks?
You,

Who La Rochelle had saved by bloody fights,
Or I, who spent in Laon peaceful nights?"
"In faith, Sire, I, who guarded La Rochelle!"
The wondering Master cried.
"So, then, I tell
Thee," said the Bishop, in most gentle tone,
"My heart is like the Castle of Laon.
Temptations, doubts, cannot my soul assail.
Therefore, I say that thou, who dost prevail
Against such foes of Satan's mustering,
Art four times pleasing to the Heavenly King,
Where I am once; and thy good fortress, kept,
Shall win thee glory such as saints have wept
To win! Go, joyful! Put thy sorrow by.
Thou art far dearer to the Lord than I."
Scarce dared the Master trust such words as these;
But silent, grateful, fell upon his knees
Until the Bishop blessed him. Then he went
Away in solemn wonder and content.

They lie in graves, the saints who knew this tale,
The King, the Bishop, and the Seneschal,
And he who doubted, — rest their souls in peace! —
And even mention of their names men cease
To make. But, knowing all, as they must know,
Of God, who roam his universes through,
Untrammelled spirits, they could tell to men
To-day no deeper truth than was told then,
To cheer and comfort him who fighteth well
To save a heart besieged like La Rochelle.

FORM.

HIDDEN secret of all things!
Thy triumph, most triumphant, brings
No sound of syllable of name
To mark the law by which it came;
The subtle point of difference,
Which made the joy of joy intense,
The grief of grief too great to bear,
Beauty than beauty's self more fair.

No skill does more, at best, than work
Blindly, in hope to find where lurk
Thy undiscovered charm and spell;
No prophecies thine hour foretell;
No hindrances thine hour avert;
No purpose brings thee good or hurt;
Thy life knows not of wish or will;
Inherent growths thy growth fulfil.

No man dared say to curve, to line,
"Be beautiful, by word of mine!
I crown thee lovely on the earth!
I am thy Lord of life and birth."
Before all men the line, the curve,
Stood suddenly, and said:
                    " Preserve
What joy ye can. O blind of eye!
Behold us once before ye die!"

O hidden secret of all things !
O kingdom earlier than kings !
Before earth was, yea, and before
The Heavens, Eternity forbore
All haste, waiting each sign and bond,
For seal of thee, to set beyond
All time's impatience the decree
And record of thy sovereignty ! "

MY HICKORY FIRE.

HELPLESS body of hickory tree,
What do I burn, in burning thee ?
Summers of sun, winters of snow,
Springs full of sap's resistless flow ;
All past year's joys of garnered fruits ;
All this year's purposed buds and shoots ;
Secrets of fields of upper air,
Secrets which stars and planets share ;
Light of such smiles as broad skies fling ;
Sound of such tunes as wild winds sing ;
Voices which told where gay birds dwelt,
Voices which told where lovers knelt ; —
O strong white body of hickory tree,
How dare I burn all these, in thee ?

But I too bring, as to a pyre,
Sweet things to feed thy funeral fire :
Memories waked by thy deep spell ;
Faces of fears and hopes which fell ;

Faces of darlings long since dead, —
Smiles that they smiled, and words they said ;
Like living shapes they come and go,
Lit by the mounting flame's red glow.
But sacredest of all, O tree,
Thou hast the hour my love gave me.
Only thy rhythmic silence stirred
While his low-whispered tones I heard ;
By thy last gleam of flickering light
I saw his cheek turn red from white ;
O cold gray ashes, side by side
With yours, that hour's sweet pulses died !

   But thou, brave tree, how do I know
That through these fires thou dost not go
As in old days the martyrs went
Through fire which was a sacrament?
How do I know thou dost not wait
In longing for thy next estate ? —
Estate of higher, nobler place,
Whose shapes no man can use or trace.
How do I know, if I could reach
The secret meaning of thy speech,
But I thy song of praise should hear,
Ringing triumphant, loud, and clear, —
The waiting angels could discern,
And token of thy heaven learn ?
O glad, freed soul of hickory tree,
Wherever thine eternity,
Bear thou with thee that hour's dear name,
Made pure, like thee, by rites of flame !

REVENUES.

I SMILE to hear the little kings
When they count up their precious things,
And send their vaunting lists abroad,
Of what their kingdoms can afford.
One boasts his corn, and one his wine,
And one his gold and silver fine;
One by an army, one by a fleet,
Keeps neighbor kings beneath his feet;
One sets his claim to highest place
On looms of silk and looms of lace;
And one shows pictures of old saints
In lifelike tints of wondrous paints;
And one has quarries of white stone
From which rare statue shapes have grown;
And so, by dint of wealth or grace,
Striving to keep the highest place,
They count and show their precious things,
The little race of little kings.

"O little kings!" I long to say,
"Who counts God's revenues to-day?
Who knows on all the hills and coasts
Names of the captains of his hosts?
What eye has seen the half of gold
His smallest mine has in its hold?
What figures tell one summer's cost
Of fabrics which are torn and tost

To clothe his myriads of trees?
Who reckons, in the sounding seas,
The shining corals, wrought and graved,
With which his ocean floors are paved?
Who knows the numbers or the names
Of colors in his sunset flames?
What table measures, marking weight,
What chemistries can estimate
One single banquet for his birds?"
Then, mocked by all which utmost words
And utmost thoughts can frame or reach,
My heart finds tears its only speech.
In ecstasy, part joy, part pain,
Where fear and wonder half restrain
Love's gratitude, I lay my ear
Close to the ground, and listening hear
This noiseless, ceaseless, boundless tide
Of earth's great wealth, on every side,
Rolling and pouring up to break
At feet of God, who will not take
Nor keep among his heavenly things
So much as tithe of all it brings;
But instant turns the costly wave,
Gives back to earth all that it gave,
Spends all his universe of power
And pomp to deck one single hour
Of time, and then in largess free,
Unasked, bestows the hour on me.

A BURIAL SERVICE.

TO this burying
    We come alone, — you and I, — not with
        our dead,
    But with our dearest living; O, could mor-
        tal tread
    Be unfaltering!

    God knows how we love it,
This we have come to bury; the eyes smile, — life's
        best wine
The hands hold out! Darling, shall it be yours, or
        mine,
    To lay the first sod above it?

    But no decaying
Can reach it in this sepulchre, whose stone
Our hearts must make! To an exceeding glory grown,
    This grief, outweighing,

    Not even regretting,
It will await us! Thank God, not being sown
In any dishonor, it will await its own,
    Never forgetting!

    To Christ's protection
Now let us leave it, — the tomb and the key! He
Will remember us, if there may ever be
    Resurrection!

A PARABLE.

AR in the wood I found a vine, so sweet
Of flower and leaf that, loving it, I stayed
To learn its secret. Thick around its feet
Grew thorny briers, and tangled saplings made
On every side of it too dark a shade.
One tendril by a dead branch held. The rest
Were folded like proud arms upon its breast.

The rough wind beat it down; it did not break,
But, lying low until the storm went by,
Lifted its head again. Still it would take
No help; but, shaking off with scornful eye
The dust, rose slowly, looking to the sky,
Borne up by hidden forces of its own,
And stood again erect, a vine, alone

Far in the wood I whispered then, afraid
The question showed not all my love, " O vine,
Brave vine, so sweet and yet so strong, what made
It easy unto thee? No sun can shine
To warm thee in this cold, unwholesome shade.
Why standest thou apart from all the rest,
Thy slender proud arms folded on thy breast?"

Filling the wood, this subtile whisper then
My reverent listening heard:

"My love, the Oak,
Has died. Never before his name to men
Who, idly questioning, passed by, I spoke.
But thou, — thou lov'st like me; thy secret woke
My own. Thou know'st to a less lordly thing
The tendrils torn from oaks will never cling."

FRIENDS.

TO

A. E. P.

E rode a day, from east, from west,
    To meet. A year had done its best,
    By absence, and by loss of speech,
    To put beyond the other's reach
Each heart and life; but, drawing nigh,
" Ah! it is you!" " Yes, it is I!"
We said; and love had been blasphemed
And slain in each had either deemed
Need of more words, or joy more plain
When eyes had looked in eyes again:
Ah friendship, stronger in thy might
Than time and space, as faith than sight!
Rich festival with thy red wine
My friend and I will keep in courts divine!

THE ROYAL BEGGAR.

MARVEL strange! outside the palace doors,
And begging humbly from the palace stores,
He stands and waits; and when a paltry crust
Is flung, he stoops and picks it from the dust,
And, smiling through his tears, clasps to his breast
The niggard boon; and, for the moment blest
And fed, is grateful, though the ruby wine
And milk and honey which, by right divine,
Are his, his only, and the crown of gold
God wrought for him, are to his rightful hold
Refused!
    Ah Love, dear Love, nowhere on earth
Wanders uncrowned thy peer of royal birth!
Ah Love, great Love! Denied, thrust out in vain,
Kingly, though beggared! Blest through all the pain!

MARCH.

ENEATH the sheltering walls the thin snow clings, —
Dead winter's skeleton, left bleaching, white,
Disjointed, crumbling, on unfriendly fields.
The inky pools surrender tardily

At noon, to patient herds, a frosty drink
From jagged rims of ice ; a subtle red
Of life is kindling every twig and stalk
Of lowly meadow growths ; the willows wrap
Their stems in furry white ; the pines grow gray
A little in the biting wind ; midday
Brings tiny burrowed creatures, peeping out
Alert for sun.
　　　　　　Ah March ! we know thou art
Kind-hearted, spite of ugly looks and threats,
And, out of sight, art nursing April's violets !

APRIL.

OBINS call robins in tops of trees ;
　　Doves follow doves, with scarlet feet ;
　Frolicking babies, sweeter than these,
　　Crowd green corners where highways
　　　meet.

Violets stir and arbutus wakes,
　Claytonia's rosy bells unfold ;
Dandelion through the meadow makes
　A royal road, with seals of gold.

Golden and snowy and red the flowers,
　Golden, snowy, and red in vain ;
Robins call robins through sad showers ;
　The white dove's feet are wet with rain.

For April sobs while these are so glad,
  April weeps while these are so gay, —
Weeps like a tired child who had,
  Playing with flowers, lost its way.

MAY.

THE voice of one who goes before to make
The paths of June more beautiful, is thine,
Sweet May ! Without an envy of her crown
And bridal ; patient stringing emeralds
And shining rubies for the brows of birch
And maple ; flinging garlands of pure white
And pink, which to their bloom add prophecy ;
Gold cups o'er-filling on a thousand hills
And calling honey-bees ; out of their sleep
The tiny summer harpers with bright wings
Awaking, teaching them their notes for noon ; —
O May, sweet-voiced one, going thus before,
Forever June may pour her warm red wine
Of life and passion, — sweeter days are thine !

THE SIMPLE KING.

THE king, the royal, simple king,
Whom in bold lovingness I sing,
Will not be buried when he dies,
 As kings are buried. Where he lies,
No regal monument will show;
No worldly pilgrim-feet will go;
No heraldry, with blazoned sign,
Will keep the record of his line.
No man will know his kingdom's bound;
No man his subjects' grief will sound.
His crown will nōt lie low with him;
His crown will never melt nor dim.

This king, this royal, simple king,
Whose kingliness I kneel to sing,
Looks on all other men with eyes
Which are as calm as suns that rise
Alike, and bring an equal gain
To just and unjust. Like soft rain
His gentle kindliness, but deep
As waters, in which oceans keep
Their treasures. Silent, warm, and white
As mid-day is his love's great light;
But in its faithful summer saves
For every smallest flower that waves
Such shelter that it cannot die
Nor droop, while love's fierce noons pass by.

THE SIMPLE KING.

This king, this royal, simple king,
Whose kingliness I cannot sing,
Speaks words which are decrees, because
They come as questions, not as laws.
Himself devoutest worshipper
At Truth's great shrine, his least acts stir
The people's hearts, as when of old
The High Priest, lifting veil of gold,
Came from the ark's most sacred place,
And only by his shining face
Revealed to them without that he
Had seen the Godhead bodily.
Men serve him; but while they obey
Feel no oppression in the sway.
His royal hand is burdened too;
No load of theirs to him is new;
No sting or stigma in a bond
To him whose vision looks beyond
All names and shapes of numbered days,
All accidents of human ways,
And, superseding signs and shrifts
Of all allegiances, lifts
Service to Freedom's regal plane
Beyond compulsion or disdain.

This king, this royal, simple king,
Whose kingliness I love and sing,
Has not much silver or much gold:
Told as kings' treasuries are told,
Beggar's estate he must confess.
But all the lavish wilderness

Sets state for him. Tall pine-trees bend;
Strange birds sing songs which never end.
The sunset and the sunrise sweep
Backward and forward swift, to keep
Fresh glory round his pathway. Then,
Of sudden men discover, when
They journey thither by his side,
What pomp and splendor are supplied
By Nature's smallest, subtlest thing,
To hail and crown the simple king.
Yea! and the dull and stony street,
And walls within which rich men meet,
Cities, and all they compass, grow
Significant, when to and fro
The simple king, unrecognized,
Unenvious, and unsurprised,
Walks smilingly, and as he treads
Unconscious benediction spreads.

Ah! king, thou royal, simple king!
Not as by any grave I sing;
Neither by any present throne;
King crowned to-day, king who hast gone,
In kingliness one and the same!
The house runs not by race or name;
No day but sees, no land but knows;
The kingdom lasts, the kingdom grows;
God holds earth dearer and more dear,
God's sons come nearer and more near.

THE SINGER'S FRIENDS.

HE roamed the earth with lonely feet;
   No homestead lured him back;
Lands are so full; life is so sweet;
Such skies and suns forever meet
To make each day's great joy complete;
   'Twas strange that he so much must lack.

'Twas stranger yet that joy could still
   His bosom overflow;
That smallest things his soul could fill
With ecstasy and song, whose thrill
No pain could hinder or could chill,
   As lonely he went to and fro.

But ever if there came a day,
   Which on his joy and song
So heavy load of sorrow lay
That heart and voice could not obey,
And feet refused the lonely way,
   So lonely, and so hard, and long,

It always chanced, — though chance is not,
   The word when God befriends, —
That on such days to him was brought
Echo from some old song, forgot,
Which sudden made his lonely lot
   Seem cast for worthier, sweeter ends.

Some stranger whose sad eyes were wet
   With tears, would take his hands,
Saying, "O Singer, my great debt
To thee I never can forget.
My grief in thy grief's words was set,
   And comforted forever stands."

Or else he heard, borne on the air
   Where merry music rang,
Making the fair day still more fair,
Lifting the burden off of care,
Old words of his that did their share,
   While happy people laughed and sang.

Or else, — O, sacredest of all,
   And sweetest recompense, —
Love used his words, its love to call
By name: of his dead joy, the thrall
Waked live joy still, and could forestall
   Love's utmost passion's subtlest sense.

So when at last, in lonely grave,
   He laid his lonely head,
No loving heart more tears need crave;
Nowhere more sacred grasses wave;
All human hearts to whom he gave
   Grieved like friends' hearts when he was dead.

DOUBT.

THEY bade me cast the thing away,
  They pointed to my hands all bleeding,
  They listened not to all my pleading;
  The thing I meant I could not say;
I knew that I should rue the day
If once I cast that thing away.

  I grasped it firm, and bore the pain;
The thorny husks I stripped and scattered;
If I could reach its heart, what mattered
  If other men saw not my gain,
  Or even if I should be slain?
I knew the risks; I chose the pain.

  O, had I cast that thing away,
I had not found what most I cherish,
A faith without which I should perish, —
  The faith which, like a kernel, lay
  Hid in the husks which on that day
My instinct would not throw away!

FORGIVEN.

DREAMED so dear a dream of you last
    night!
I thought you came. I was so glad, so gay,
I whispered, "Those were foolish words
    to say:
I meant them not. I cannot bear the sight
Of your dear face. I cannot meet the light
Of your dear eyes upon me. Sit, I pray, —
Sit here beside me : turn your look away,
And lay your cheek on mine." Till morning bright
We sat so, and we did not speak. I knew
All was forgiven ; so I nestled there   [flew.
With your arms round me. Swift the sweet hours
At last I waked, and sought you everywhere.
How long, dear, think you, that my glad cheek will
Burn, — as it burns with your cheek's pressure still?

THIS SUMMER.

THOUGHT I knew all Summer knows,
    So many summers I had been
    Wed to Summer. Could I suppose
        One hidden beauty still lurked in
Her days? that she might still disclose
    New secrets, and new homage win?

Could new looks flit across the skies?
    Could water ripple one new sound?

Could stranger bee or bird that flies
    With yet new languages be found,
To bring me, to my glad surprise,
    Message from yet remoter bound?

O sweet " this Summer ! " Songs which sang
    Summer before no longer mean
The whole of summer. Bells which rang
    But minutes have marked years between.
Purple the grapes of Autumn hang:
    My sweet " this Summer " still is green.

" This Summer " still, — forgetting all
    Before and since and aye, — I say,
And shall say, when the deep snows fall,
    And cold suns mark their shortest day.
New calendar, my heart will call;
    " This Summer " still ! Summer alway !

And when God's next sweet world we reach,
    And the poor words we stammered here
Are fast forgot, while angels teach
    Us spirit language quick and clear,
Perhaps some words of earthly speech
    We still shall speak, and still hold dear.

And if some time in upper air
    On swiftest wings we sudden meet,
And pause with answering smiles which share
    Our joy, I think that we shall greet
Each other thus : " This world is fair ;
    But ah ! that Summer too was sweet ! "

TRYST.

SOMEWHERE thou awaitest,
   And I, with lips unkissed,
Weep that thus to latest
   Thou puttest off our tryst!

The golden bowls are broken,
   The silver cords untwine;
Almond flowers in token
   Have bloomed, — that I am thine!

Others who would fly thee
   In cowardly alarms,
Who hate thee and deny thee,
   Thou foldest in thine arms!

How shall I entreat thee
   No longer to withhold?
I dare not go to meet thee,
   O lover, far and cold!

O lover, whose lips chilling
   So many lips have kissed,
Come, even if unwilling,
   And keep thy solemn tryst!

THE MAGIC ARMORY.

No man can shut the open door;
Strange hieroglyphs of mystic lore
Are writ on it from beam to sill;
The gleams and shapes of weapons fill
Its silent chambers: field and fray
Of centuries have borne away
Its armor to their victories,
And yet to-day the armor lies
Unstained and bright and whole and good,
For each man's utmost hardihood.

All men go freely out and in,
And choose their arms to fight and win;
But one man goes with silly hands,
And helpless, halting, choosing stands,
And from the glittering, deadly steels,
Fits him with clumsy sword, and deals
A feeble, witless, useless blow,
Which hurts no friend and helps no foe.
Close by his side his brother makes
Swift choice, unerringly, and takes
From those same chambers hilt and blade
With which more magic sword is made
Than that far-famed which armed the hand
Of Lion-Heart in Eastern land.

So fight and fray the centuries,
The right and truth with wrong and lies;

So men go freely out and in,
And choose their arms, and lose and win;
And none can shut the open door,
All writ with signs of mystic lore,
Where weapons stout and old and good
For each man's utmost hardihood
Lie ready, countless, priceless, free,
Within the magic armory.

LIFTED OVER.

AS tender mothers guiding baby steps,
   When places come at which the tiny feet
   Would trip, lift up the little ones in arms
   Of love, and set them down beyond the harm,
So did Our Father watch the precious boy,
Led o'er the stones by me, who stumbled of
Myself, but strove to help my darling on :
He saw the sweet limbs faltering, and saw
Rough ways before us, where my arms would fail ;
So reached from heaven, and lifting the dear child,
Who smiled in leaving me, He put him down
Beyond all hurt, beyond my sight, and bade
Him wait for me ! Shall I not then be glad,
And, thanking God, press on to overtake ?

MY HOUSE NOT MADE WITH HANDS.

T is so old, the date is dim ;
I hear the wise man vexing him
With effort vain to count and read,
But to his words I give small heed,
Except of pity that so late
He sitteth wrangling in the gate,
When he might come with me inside,
And in such peace and plenty bide.
The constant springs and summers thatch,
With leaves that interlock and match,
Such roof as keeps out fiercest sun
And gentle rain, but one by one
Lets in blue banner-gleams of sky
As pomp of day goes marching by
Under these roofs I lie whole days,
Watching the steady household ways :
Innumerable creatures come
And go, and are far more at home
Than I, who like dumb giant sit
Baffled by all their work and wit.
No smallest of them condescends
To notice me ; their hidden ends
They follow, and above, below,
Across my bulky shape they go,
With swift, sure feet, and subtle eyes,
Too keen and cautious for surprise
In vain I try their love to reach ;

Not one will give me trust or speech.
No second look the furry bee
Gives, as he bustles round, to me ;
Before my eyes slim spiders take
Their silken ladders out and make
No halt, no secret, scaling where
They like, and weaving scaffolds there ;
The beaded ants prick out and in,
Mysterious and dark and thin ;
With glittering spears and gauzy mail
Legions of insects dart and sail,
Swift Bedouins of the pathless air,
Finding rich plunder everywhere ;
Sweet birds, with motion more serene
Than stillest rest, soar up between
The fleecy clouds, then, sinking slow,
Light on my roof. I do not know
That they are there till fluttering
Low sounds, like the unravelling
Of tight-knit web, their soft wings make,
Unfurling further flight to take.
All through my house is set out food,
Ready and plenty, safe and good,
In vessels made of cunning shapes,
Whose liquid spicy sweet escapes
By drops at brims of yellow bowls,
Or tips of trumpets red as coals,
Or cornucopias pink and white,
By millions set in circles tight ;
Red wine turned jelly, and in moulds
Of pointed calyx laid on folds

Of velvet green; fruit-grains of brown,
Like dusty shower thickly strewn
On underside of fronds, and hid
Unless one lift the carven lid;
And many things which in my haste
And ignorance I reckon waste,
Unsightly and unclean, I find
Are but delicious food, designed
For travellers who come each day,
And eat, and drink, and go their way.
I am the only one who need
Go hungry where so many feed;
My birthright of protection lost,
Because of fathers' sins the cost
Is counted in the children's blood:
I starve where once I might have stood
Content and strong as bird or bee,
Feeding like them on flower or tree.
When I have hunger, I must rise
And seek the poisons I despise,
Leaving untouched on every hand
The sweet wild foods of air and land,
And leaving all my happier kin
Of beasts and birds behind to win
The great rewards which only they
Can win who Nature's laws obey.

Under these roofs of waving thatch,
Lying whole days to dream and watch,
I find myself grow more and more
Vassal of summer than before;

Allegiances I thought were sworn
For life I break with hate and scorn.
One thing alone I hope, desire:
To make my human life come nigher
The life these lead whose silent gaze
Reproaches me and all my ways;
To glide along as they all glide,
Submissive and unterrified,
Without a thought of loss or gain,
Without a jar of haste or pain,
And go, without one quickened breath,
Finding all realms of life, of death,
But summer hours in sunny lands,
To my next house not made with hands.

MY STRAWBERRY.

O MARVEL, fruit of fruits, I pause
To reckon thee. I ask what cause
Set free so much of red from heats
At core of earth, and mixed such sweets
With sour and spice: what was that strength
Which out of darkness, length by length,
Spun all thy shining thread of vine,
Netting the fields in bond as thine.
I see thy tendrils drink by sips
From grass and clover's smiling lips;
I hear thy roots dig down for wells,
Tapping the meadow's hidden cells;
Whole generations of green things,

Descended from long lines of springs,
I see make room for thee to bide
A quiet comrade by their side;
I see the creeping peoples go
Mysterious journeys to and fro,
Treading to right and left of thee,
Doing thee homage wonderingly.
I see the wild bees as they fare,
Thy cups of honey drink, but spare.
I mark thee bathe and bathe again
In sweet uncalendared spring rain.
I watch how all May has of sun
Makes haste to have thy ripeness done,
While all her nights let dews escape
To set and cool thy perfect shape.
Ah, fruit of fruits, no more I pause
To dream and seek thy hidden laws!
I stretch my hand and dare to taste,
In instant of delicious waste
On single feast, all things that went
To make the empire thou hast spent.

TRIUMPH.

NOT he who rides through conquered city's
    gate,
  At head of blazoned hosts, and to the sound
  Of victors' trumpets, in full pomp and state
Of war, the utmost pitch has dreamed or found
To which the thrill of triumph can be wound;

Nor he, who by a nation's vast acclaim
Is sudden sought and singled out alone,
And while the people madly shout his name,
Without a conscious purpose of his own,
Is swung and lifted to the nation's throne;

But he who has all single-handed stood
With foes invisible on every side,
And, unsuspected of the multitude,
The force of fate itself has dared, defied,
And conquered silently.
                      Ah that soul knows
In what white heat the blood of triumph glows!

RETURN TO THE HILLS.

LIKE a music of triumph and joy
   Sounds the roll of the wheels,
And the breath of the engine laughs out
   In loud chuckles and peals,
Like the laugh of a man that is glad
   Coming homeward at night;
I lean out of the window and nod
   To the left and the right,
To my friends in the fields and the woods;
   Not a face do I miss;
The sweet asters and browned golden-rod,
   And that stray clematis,
Of all vagabonds dearest and best,
   In most seedy estate;

I am sure they all recognize me ;
  If I only could wait,
I should hear all the welcome which now
  In their faces I read,
"O true lover of us and our kin,
  We all bid thee God speed!"

O my mountains, no wisdom can teach
  Me to think that ye care
Nothing more for my steps than the rest,
  Or that they can have share
Such as mine in your royal crown-lands,
  Unencumbered of fee;
In your temples with altars unhewn,
  Where redemption is free;
In your houses of treasure, which gold
  Cannot buy if it seek;
And your oracles, mystic with words,
  Which men lose if they speak!

Ah! with boldness of lovers who wed
  I make haste to your feet,
And as constant as lovers who die,
  My surrender repeat;
And I take as the right of my love,
  And I keep as its sign,
An ineffable joy in each sense
  And new strength as from wine,
A seal for all purpose and hope,
  And a pledge of full light,
Like a pillar of cloud for my day,
  And of fire for my night.

"DOWN TO SLEEP."

NOVEMBER woods are bare and still;
November days are clear and bright;
Each noon burns up the morning's chill;
The morning's snow is gone by night;
Each day my steps grow slow, grow light,
As through the woods I reverent creep,
Watching all things lie " down to sleep."

I never knew before what beds,
Fragrant to smell, and soft to touch,
The forest sifts and shapes and spreads;
I never knew before how much
Of human sound there is in such
Low tones as through the forest sweep
When all wild things lie " down to sleep."

Each day I find new coverlids
Tucked in, and more sweet eyes shut tight;
Sometimes the viewless mother bids
Her ferns kneel down, full in my sight;
I hear their chorus of " good night ";
And half I smile, and half I weep,
Listening while they lie " down to sleep."

November woods are bare and still;
November days are bright and good;
Life's noon burns up life's morning chill;

Life's night rests feet which long have stood ;
Some warm soft bed, in field or wood,
The mother will not fail to keep,
Where we can "lay us down to sleep."

FALLOW.

ABOVE, below me, on the hill,
    Great fields of grain their fulness fill ;
    The golden fruit bends down the trees ;
    The grass stands high round mowers' knees ;
The bee pants through the clover-beds,
And cannot taste of half the heads ;
The farmer stands, with greedy eyes,
And counts his harvest's growing size.

Among his fields, so fair to see,
He takes no count, no note, of me.
I lie and bask, along the hill,
Content and idle, idle still,
My lazy silence never stirred
By breathless bee or hungry bird :
All creatures know the cribs which yield ;
No creature seeks the fallow field.

But to no field on all the hill
Come sun and rain with more good-will ;
All secrets which they bear and bring

To wheat before its ripening,
To clover turning purple red,
To grass in bloom for mowers' tread, —
They tell the same to my bare waste,
But never once bid me to haste.

Winter is near, and snow is sweet;
Who knows if they be seeds of wheat
Or clover, which my bosom fill?
Who knows how many summers will
Be needed, spent, before one thing
Is ready for my harvesting?
And after all, if all were laid
Into sure balances and weighed,
Who knows if all the gain and get
On which hot human hearts are set
Do more than mark the drought and dearth
Through which this little dust of earth
Must lie and wait in God's great hand,
A patient bit of fallow land?

LOVE'S RICH AND POOR.

TAKING me hand in hand,
Love led me through his land.
His land bloomed white and red;
His palaces were fair;
Glad people everywhere
Stood smiling.
   Then Love said, —

"With all my kingdom wins,
Never my heart begins
To rest; my cruel poor
So rob my rich. By speech,
By look, they overreach,
And plunder every store.

"My rich I love, and make
More rich, for giving's sake.
My poor I scorn; they choose
Their chilly beggary;
My gold is ready, free,
But they forget, refuse.

"My rich I love. I weep
To see them starved, to keep
My worthless poor well fed;
To see them shiver, cold,
While wrapped with fold on fold,
The beggars sleep in bed.

"My rich I love, and yet
My love no law can set;
In vain I warn and cry;
They give, and give, and give;
The selfish beggars live,
And smiling see them die."

Then walking hand in hand
With Love throughout his land, —
Land blooming white and red, —
I saw that everywhere,
Where life and love looked fair,
It was as he had said.

LIGHT ON THE MOUNTAIN-TOPS.

N Alpine valleys, they who watch for dawn
Look never to the east; but fix their eyes
On loftier mountain-peaks of snow, which rise
To west or south. Before the happy morn
Has sent one ray of kindling red, to warn
The sleeping clouds along the eastern skies
That it is near, — flushing, in glad surprise,
These royal hills, for royal watchmen born,
Discover that God's great new day begins,
And, shedding from their sacred brows a light
Prophetic, wake the valley from its night.

Such mystic light as this a great soul wins,
Who overlooks earth's wall of griefs and sins,
And steadfast, always, gazing on the white
Great throne of God, can call aloud with deep,
Pure voice of truth, to waken them who sleep.

BAD-GASTEIN, AUSTRIA, September 9, 1869.

CHRISTMAS NIGHT IN ST. PETER'S.

NOW on the marble floor I lie :
    I am alone :
Though friendly voices whisper nigh,
And foreign crowds are passing by,
  I am alone.
  Great hymns float through
The shadowed aisles. I hear a slow
Refrain, " Forgive them, for they know
    Not what they do."

With tender joy all others thrill ;
    I have but tears :
The false priests' voices, high and shrill,
Reiterate the " Peace, good-will " ;
    I have but tears.
    I hear anew
The nails and scourge ; then come the low
Sad words, " Forgive them, for they know
    Not what they do."

Close by my side the poor souls kneel;
    I turn away;
Half-pitying looks at me they steal;
They think, because I do not feel,
    I turn away.
    Ah! if they knew,
How following them, where'er they go,
I hear, "Forgive them, for they know
    Not what they do"

Above the organ's sweetest strains
    I hear the groans
Of prisoners, who lie in chains,
So near, and in such mortal pains,
    I hear the groans.
    But Christ walks through
The dungeons of St. Angelo,
And says, "Forgive them, for they know
    Not what they do."

And now the music sinks to sighs;
    The lights grow dim:
The Pastorella's melodies
In lingering echoes float and rise;
    The lights grow dim;
    More clear and true,
In this sweet silence, seem to flow
The words, "Forgive them, for they know
    Not what they do."

The dawn swings incense, silver gray;
    The night is past;

Now comes, triumphant, God's full day ;
No priest, no church can bar its way :
　　The night is past :
　　How, on this blue
Of God's great banner, blaze and glow
The words, " Forgive them, for they know
　　Not what they do ! "

ROME, December 26, 1868.

WELCOME.

TO C. C.

WELCOME! Perhaps the simple word says
　　all.
And yet, when from a country's earnest heart
It sudden springs, quick pride and triumph
　　start,
Eager as love, and even hold in thrall
Of silence love's own speech, while they recall
How in all men's great deeds of life and art
Their native land immortal share and part
Must keep.　　　But thou, O royal soul, how small
Such laurels unto thee, we know who love
Thee, and whom thou hast loved ! We dare to bring
To thee this mite of silent offering,
And know how it thy great, warm heart will move,
That, dumb with joy, we find no voice as yet,
And cannot see, because our eyes are wet !

TWO COMRADES.

To O. W. and H. de K.

S when in some green forest depth we find
The spot to which with idle, tinkling feet,
Two brooks have danced all unawares to meet
Each other, where at sight they interwind
Their shining arms, and loving, trusting, bind
Themselves for life, and with a louder song
And in a wider channel glide along;

As when in some great symphony we trace,
Through deep and underlying harmonies,
How all the notes of melody uprise,
Lifted by answering notes in distant place,
Fulfilling each in each the final grace,
But shielding, keeping each from each
The separate voices through the blended speech;

So when we see two human souls by fate
Held in life's restless current side by side,
And in their deepest nature so allied
That each, but for the other, life's estate
Must smaller find, a sense of joy, too great
Almost for speech, thrills earnest souls who heed
Their fellowship and long to say "God-speed!"

TWO COMRADES.

Two comrades such as these I know, — young, fair;
So fair, that choice cannot find right to choose;
So fair, that wish can nothing miss or lose
In either face; so young, their eyes still wear
The looks with which young children trust and dare;
So young, the womanhood of each warm heart
As yet finds love enough in love of Art.

One, silent, — with a silence whose quick speech
By subtler eloquence than any word,
Reveals when deepest depths are touched and
    stirred, —
Reveals by color tides which mount and reach
Her broad, white brow, as on some magic beach,
Where only spotless, peaceful snows resist,
Might break a crimson sea through veiling mist.

Silent, with silence which might often make
Dull ears believe the answer unexpressed
Meant an assent, or aquiescent rest;
Silence whose earnestness dull souls mistake;
But silence out of which words leap and break,
As from their sheaths swords leap and flash in sun,
When comes the time for swords, and truce is done;

Silence which to all finer spirits is
Full of such revelation and delight
As Nature's lovers find and feel in sight
Of her most sacred, subtle silences;
Silence of mountain lake, untouched by breeze;
Silence of lily's heart, cool, white, and pure;
Silence of crystal growths, patient and sure.

The other, earnest equally, but born
With veins made for a tropic current's flow;
Intolerant if fate seem cold, seem slow;
Full of a noble, restless, dauntless scorn;
Unjust to night, for eager love of morn;
Unjust to small things for the love of great;
Too faithless of all good which tarries late.

But yet through all this tropic current's heat,
Through all this scorn of failures and delays,
Lives faithfulness which never disobeys
The smallest law of patience, and, more sweet
Than patience' self, works on to its complete
Fulfilling, wresting thus from alien powers
A double guerdon for the conquered hours.

In vain among all rich and beauteous things
With which the realms of beauteous Nature teems
I look for one which fair and fitting seems
As simile for her swift soul, which wings
Itself more swift than bird can fly, which springs
And soars like fountain, but finds no content
At levels whence its own bright waters went.

Only one thing there is whose name is name
Also for her: swift, restless, patient fire,
Which, burning always, loses no desire;
Which leaps and soars and blazes all the same,
If spices or dull fagots feed its flame;
Swift, restless, patient fire, which saves and turns
Into more precious things all things it burns.

O comrades, sweet to know and hear and see,
Whom I have dared to paint, each empty phrase
But mocks my thought; no dreamy singer's praise,
No flattering voice of hope and prophecy
Of what the future years shall bring and be,
No stranger's recognition do ye need!
Ah! comrades, sweet to hear and see, "God-speed!"

DEMETER.

 LEGEND of foul shame to motherhood!
How doubly orphaned ignorance which wrought
Such tale; which deemed a mother's soul had bought
One healing for her woe in that she could
Strike other mothers desolate; — made good
Her loss by theirs, unpitying while they sought
As she had sought, weeping and finding nought
But cruel empty places where had stood
The children. Ah, true motherhood, bereft,
Finds only joy in thought that joy is left
For other mothers: smiling, it abides
In loneliness, a little way apart,
And from all happy mothers gladly hides,
And veils the chilly winter in its heart.

EXPECTANCY.

PERPETUAL dawn makes glorious all hills;
Perpetual altar-feast sets fresh shew-bread;
Perpetual symphony swells overhead;
Perpetual revelation pours and fills
For every eye and ear and soul which wills
And waits, with will and waiting which are wed
Into true harmony, like that which led
The forces under which, with silent thrills,
Earth's subtile life began.
      Ah, on the brink
Of each new age of great eternity, I think,
After the ages have all countless grown,
Our souls will poise and launch with eager wing,
Forgetting blessedness already known,
In sweet impatience for God's next good thing.

BELATED.

ON a September day I came
Seeking that flower of sweetest name
Of all, from which the lavish June
With boundless fragrance fills the noon,
In woods where her best blossoms hide.
"O sweet Twin-Flower!" I longing cried,
Hopeless but eager, "is there still
One tiny pink bell left? And will

BELATED.

Thy guardian fairy condescend
To guide my feet, that I may bend,
In reverent and fond delight,
Once more at the transcendent sight?"
The spicy woods were still and cool;
In many a little mossy pool
Bright leaves were floating round and round;
The partridge mother's watchful sound,
The sighs of dying leaves that fell,
Were all that broke the silent spell.
In mats and tangles everywhere,
The Twin-Flower vines lay, green and fair,
With subtle beauty all their own,
Wreathing each hillock and each stone,
Stretching in slender coiling shoot,
Far out of sight of parent root,
Making white silken fibres fast
To all the mosses as they passed;
But trembling, empty, withered, bare,
Stood all the thread-like flower-stems there.
"Too late," I said, and rambled on,
Sadder because the flowers were gone,
Yet glad, and laden with green vines
Of everything that climbs and twines;
With glossy ferns, and snowy seeds
Strung thick on scarlet stems, like beads,
And Tiarellas packed between
In mottled, scalloped disks of green,
And purple Asters fit for hem
Of High-Priest's robes, and, shading them
Like sunlit tree-tops waving broad,
Great branching stalks of Golden Rod.

So, glad and laden, through the wood
I went, till on its edge I stood,
When at my very feet I saw,
With sudden joy, half joy, half awe,
Low nestled in a dead log's cleft
One pale Twin-Flower, the last one left.
So near my hasty step had been
To trampling it, it quivered in
The air, and like a fairy bell
Swung to and fro, with notes that fell
No doubt on hidden ears more fine,
And more of kin to it than mine.
"O dear belated thing!" I cried,
And knelt like worshipper beside
The mossy log. The wood, so still,
With sudden echo seemed to fill.
Repeated on each side I heard
In soft rebuke my thoughtless word,
" Belated "!
    No! ah, never yet
The smallest reckoning was set
Too slow, too fast, by Nature's hand.
Her hours appointed faithful stand.
Her million doors wide-open stay.
Love cannot lose nor leave his way,
Comes not too soon, comes not too late.
Twin-Flowers and hearts their lovers wait.

TO AN UNKNOWN LADY.

There lived a lady who was lovelier
   Than anything that my poor skill may paint, —
   Though I would follow round the world till faint
I fell, for just one little look at her.
Who said she seemed like this or that did err:
   Like her dear self she was, alone, — no taint
   From touch of mortal or of earth ; blest saint
Serene, with many a faithful worshipper!
   There is no poet's poesy would not,
When laid against the whiteness of her meek,
   Proud, solemn face, make there a pitiful blot.
It is so strange that I can never speak
   Of her without a tear. O, I forgot!
This surely may fall blameless on that cheek!

From THE RIDDLE OF LOVERS, *Scribner's Monthly for June,* 1873.

   KNOW a lady — no, I do not know
      Her face, her voice; I do not know her name :
      And yet such sudden, subtle knowledge came
To me of her one day, that I am slow
To think that if I met her I should go
   Amiss in greeting her. Such sweet, proud shame
   In every look would tell her hidden fame
Whose poet lover, singing, loves her so
   That all his songs unconsciously repeat
The fact of her, no matter what he sings,

The color and the tone of her in things
　Remotest, and the presence of her, sweet
　And strong to hold him lowest at her feet,
When most he soars on highest sunlit wings.

I bless thee, Lady whom I do not know!
　I thank God for thy unseen, beauteous face,
　And lovely soul, which make this year of grace
In all our land so full of grace to grow;
As years were, solemn centuries ago,
　When lovers knew to set in stateliest place
　Their mistresses, and, for their sake, no race
Disdained or feared to run, they loved them so.
　Reading the verses which I know are thine,
My heart grows reverent, as on holy ground.
　I think of many an unnamed saintly shrine
I saw in Old World churches, hung around
　With pictured scrolls and gifts in grateful sign
Of help which sore-pressed souls of men had found.

O sweetest immortality, which pain
　Of Love's most bitter ecstasy can buy,
　Sole immortality which can defy
Earth's power on earth's own ground, and never wane
All other ways, hearts breaking, try in vain.
　All fire and flood and moth and rust outvie
　Love's artifice. The sculptor's marbles lie
In shapeless fragments; and to dust again
　The painter's hand had scarcely turned, before
His colors faded. But the poet came,

Giving to her from whom he took, his fame,
  Placing her than the angels little lower,
  And centuries cannot harm her any more
Than they can pale the stars which heard her name.

A WILD ROSE IN SEPTEMBER.

WILD red rose, what spell has stayed
    Till now thy summer of delights?
  Where hid the south wind when he laid
    His heart on thine, these autumn nights?

O wild red rose! Two faces glow
  At sight of thee, and two hearts share
All thou and thy south wind can know
  Of sunshine in this autumn air.

O sweet wild rose! O strong south wind!
  The sunny roadside asks no reasons
Why we such secret summer find,
  Forgetting calendars and seasons!

Alas! red rose, thy petals wilt;
  Our loving hands tend thee in vain;
Our thoughtless touch seems like a guilt;
  Ah, could we make thee live again!

Yet joy, wild rose! Be glad, south wind!
  Immortal wind! immortal rose!
Ye shall live on, in two hearts shrined,
  With secrets which no words disclose.

AN ARCTIC QUEST.

PROUDLY name their names who bravely
    sail
To seek brave lost in Arctic snows and seas!
Bring money and bring ships, and on strong
    knees
Pray prayers so strong that not one word can fail
To pierce God's listening heart!
                    Rigid and pale,
The lost men's bodies, waiting, drift and freeze;
Yet shall their solemn dead lips tell to these
Who find them secrets mighty to prevail
On farther, darker, icier seas.
                    I go
Alone, unhelped, unprayed-for. Perishing
For years in realms of more than Arctic snow,
My heart has lingered.
                    Will the poor dead thing
Be sign to guide past bitter flood and floe,
To open sea, some strong heart triumphing?

THE SIGN OF THE DAISY.

ALL summer she scattered the daisy leaves;
    They only mocked her as they fell.
    She said: "The daisy but deceives;
    There is no virtue in its spell.
'He loves me not,' 'he loves me well,'
    One story no two daisies tell."
Ah, foolish heart, which waits and grieves
    Under the daisy's mocking spell!

But summer departed, and came again.
    The daisies whitened every hill;
Her heart had lost its last year's pain,
    Her heart of love had had its fill,
And held love's secrets at its will.
    The daisies stood untouched and still,
No message in that snowy rain
    To one whose heart had had its fill!

So never the daisy's sweet sign deceives,
    Though no two will one story tell;
The glad heart sees the daisy leaves,
    But thinks not of their hidden spell,
Heeds not which lingered and which fell.
    "He loves mé; yes, he loves me well."
Ah, happy heart which sees, believes!
    This is the daisy's secret spell!

VINTAGE.

BEFORE the time of grapes,
    While they altered in the sun,
And out of the time of grapes,
    When vintage songs were done, —

From secret southern spot,
    Whose warmth not a mortal knew;
From shades which the sun forgot,
    Or could not struggle through, —

Wine sweeter than first wine,
    She gave him by drop, by drop;
Wine stronger than seal could sign,
    She poured and did not stop.

Soul of my soul, the shapes
    Of the things of earth are one;
Rememberest thou the grapes
    I brought thee in the sun?

And darest thou still drink
    Wine stronger than seal can sign?
And smilest thou to think
    Eternal vintage thine?

LAST WORDS.

DEAR hearts, whose love has been so sweet
   to know,
   That I am looking backward as I go,
   Am lingering while I haste, and in this rain
Of tears of joy am mingling tears of pain;
Do not adorn with costly shrub, or tree,
Or flower, the little grave which shelters me.
Let the wild wind-sown seeds grow up unharmed,
And back and forth all summer, unalarmed,
Let all the tiny, busy creatures creep;
Let the sweet grass its last year's tangles keep;
And when, remembering me, you come some day
And stand there, speak no praise, but only say,
"How she loved us! 'T was that which made her
   dear!"
Those are the words that I shall joy to hear.

SONNETS AND LYRICS

SONNETS AND LYRICS

BY

HELEN JACKSON (H. H.)

AUTHOR OF

"VERSES," "RAMONA," "BITS OF TRAVEL," ETC., ETC.

BOSTON
ROBERTS BROTHERS
1888

Copyright, 1886,
BY ROBERTS BROTHERS.

University Press:
JOHN WILSON AND SON, CAMBRIDGE.

UNTO one who lies at rest
   'Neath the sunset, in the West,
Clover-blossoms on her breast.

Lover of each gracious thing
Which makes glad the summer-tide,
From the daisies clustering
And the violets purple-eyed,
To those shy and hidden blooms
Which in forest coverts stay,
Sending wandering perfumes
Out as guides to show the way,
All she knew, to all was kind;
None so humble or so small
That she did not seek and find
Silent friendship from them all.
Moss-cups, tiarella leaves,
Dappled like the adder's skin,
Fungus huts with ivory eaves
Which the fairies harbor in,
Regiments of fronded ferns,
Golden-rod and asters frail,
Every flaming leaf that burns
Red against the autumn pale,
Every pink-cupped wayside rose,—
All to her were dear and known;
But above them all she chose
Clover-blossoms for her own.

So they laid her to her rest
In the sun-warmed, bounteous West,
Clover-blossoms on her breast.

CONTENTS.

	PAGE
A Dream	7
Danger	9
Freedom	10
The Gods said Love is Blind	11
The Fir-Tree and the Brook	12
A Rose-Leaf	14
A Woman's Battle	15
Esther	16
Vashti	17
Burnt Offering	18
Bon Voyage	20
New Year's Morning	21
January	23
February	24
March	25
April	26
May	27

CONTENTS.

	PAGE
June	28
July	29
August	30
September	31
October	32
November	33
December	34
Refrain	35
To an Absent Lover	38
Crossed Threads	39
Outward Bound	40
Sealed Orders	41
Two	42
The Gift of Grapes	44
Avalanches	51
A Woman's Death-Wound	52
Chance	53
September	54
Appeal	56
Wreck	57
The Heart of a Rose	58
Acquainted with Grief	59
Fealty	61
Vision	62
The Poet's Forge	63
Vanity of Vanities	65

CONTENTS.

	PAGE
Morn	67
Quatrains	68
Release	70
Where?	71
Emigravit	72
My Tenants	73
The Story of Boon	75
The Victory of Patience	94
God's Light-Houses	95
Songs of Battle	97
No Man's Land	98
Just out of Sight	100
September Woods	102
To-day	105
Opportunity	106
Flowers on a Grave	107
A Measure of Hours	109
Charlotte Cushman	112
Dedication	114
Dawn	115
Eve	115
Dreams	116
The Day-Star in the East	117
October's Bright Blue Weather	119
The Riviera	121
Semitones	122

CONTENTS.

	PAGE
IN THE DARK	123
MORDECAI	124
IN APRIL	125
TWO HARVESTS	127
HABEAS CORPUS	129
A LAST PRAYER	132
THE SONG HE NEVER WROTE	133

A DREAM.

 DREAMED that I was dead and crossed
    the heavens,—
Heavens after heavens with burning feet
    and swift,—
And cried: "O God, where art Thou? I left one
On earth, whose burden I would pray Thee lift."

I was so dead I wondered at no thing,—
    Not even that the angels slowly turned
Their faces, speechless, as I hurried by
    (Beneath my feet the golden pavements burned);

Nor, at the first, that I could not find God,
    Because the heavens stretched endlessly like
        space.
At last a terror seized my very soul;
    I seemed alone in all the crowded place.

Then, sudden, one compassionate cried out,
  Though like the rest his face from me he turned,
As I were one no angel might regard
  (Beneath my feet the golden pavements burned):

"No more in heaven than earth will he find God
  Who does not know his loving mercy swift
But waits the moment consummate and ripe,
  Each burden from each human soul to lift."

Though I was dead, I died again for shame;
  Lonely, to flee from heaven again I turned;
The ranks of angels looked away from me
  (Beneath my feet the golden pavements burned).

DANGER.

WITH what a childish and short-sighted sense
Fear seeks for safety; reckons up the days
Of danger and escape, the hours and ways
Of death; it breathless flies the pestilence;
It walls itself in towers of defence;
By land, by sea, against the storm it lays
Down barriers; then, comforted, it says:
"This spot, this hour is safe." Oh, vain pretence!
Man born of man knows nothing when he goes;
The winds blow where they list, and will disclose
To no man which brings safety, which brings risk.
The mighty are brought low by many a thing
Too small to name. Beneath the daisy's disk
Lies hid the pebble for the fatal sling.

FREEDOM.

HAT freeman knoweth freedom? Never he
    Whose father's fathers through long lives have reigned
O'er kingdoms which mere heritage attained.
Though from his youth to age he roam as free
As winds, he dreams not freedom's ecstasy.
But he whose birth was in a nation chained
For centuries; where every breath was drained
From breasts of slaves which knew not there could be
Such thing as freedom, — he beholds the light
Burst, dazzling; though the glory blind his sight
He knows the joy. Fools laugh because he reels
And wields confusedly his infant will;
The wise man watching with a heart that feels
Says: "Cure for freedom's harms is freedom still."

THE GODS SAID LOVE IS BLIND.

THE gods said Love is blind. The earth was young
With foolish, youthful laughter when it heard;
It caught and spoke the letter of the words,
And from that time till now hath said and sung,
" Oh, Love is blind! The falsest face and tongue
Can cheat him, once his passion's thrill is stirred:
He is so blind, poor Love!"
        Strange none demurred
At this, nor saw how hollow false it rang,
When all men know that sightless men can tell
Unnumbered things which vision cannot find.
Powers of the air are leagued to guide them well;
And things invisible weave clew and spell
By which all labyrinths they safely wind.
Ah, we were lost, if Love had not been blind!

THE FIR-TREE AND THE BROOK.

THE Fir-Tree looked on stars, but loved the
    Brook!
"O silver-voiced! if thou wouldst wait,
My love can bravely woo." All smiles forsook
The Brook's white face. "Too late!
Too late! I go to wed the sea.
I know not if my love would curse or bless thee.
I may not, dare not, tarry to caress thee,
Oh, do not follow me!"

The Fir-Tree moaned and moaned till spring;
Then laughed in maniac joy to feel
Early one day, the woodmen of the King
Sign him with sign of burning steel,
The first to fall. "Now flee
Thy swiftest, Brook! Thy love may curse or bless
    me,
I care not, if but once thou dost caress me,
O Brook, I follow thee!"

All torn and bruised with mark of axe and chain,
Hurled down the dizzy slide of sand,

Tossed by great waves in ecstasy of pain,
And rudely thrown at last to land,
The Fir-Tree heard: "Oh, see
With what fierce love it is I must caress thee!
I warned thee I might curse, and never bless thee,
Why did'st thou follow me?"

All stately set with spar and brace and rope,
The Fir-Tree stood and sailed, and sailed.
In wildest storm when all the ship lost hope,
The Fir-Tree never shook nor quailed,
Nor ceased from saying, "Free
Art thou, O Brook! But once thou hast caressed
    me;
For life, for death, thy love has cursed or blessed
    me;
Behold, I follow thee!"

Lost in a night, and no man left to tell,
Crushed in the giant icebergs' play,
The ship went down without a song, a knell.
Still drifts the Fir-Tree night and day;
Still moans along the sea
A voice: "O Fir-Tree! thus must I possess thee;
Eternally, brave love, will I caress thee,
Dead for the love of me!"

A ROSE-LEAF.

 A ROSE-LEAF on the snowy deck,
   The high wind whirling it astern;
Nothing the wind could know or reck;
   Why did the King's eye thither turn?

"The Queen has walked here!" hoarse he cried.
   The courtiers, stunned, turned red, turned white;
No use if they had stammered, lied;
   Aghast they fled his angry sight.

Kings' wives die quick, when kings go mad;
   To death how fair and grave she goes!
What if the king knew now, she had
   Shut in her hand a little rose?

And men die quick when kings have said;
   Bleeding, dishonored, flung apart
In outcast field a man lies dead
   With rose-leaves warm upon his heart.

A WOMAN'S BATTLE.

DEAR foe, I know thou 'lt win the fight.
    I know thou hast the stronger bark,
    And thou art sailing in the light,
While I am creeping in the dark.
Thou dost not dream that I am crying,
As I come up with colors flying.

I clear away my wounded, slain,
    With strength like frenzy, strong and swift;
I do not feel the tug and strain,
    Though dead are heavy, hard to lift.
If I looked in their faces dying,
I could not keep my colors flying.

Dear foe, it will be short, — our fight, —
    Though lazily thou train'st thy guns;
Fate steers us, — me to deeper night,
    And thee to brighter seas and suns;
But thou 'lt not dream that I am dying,
As I sail by with colors flying!

ESTHER.

A FACE more vivid than he dreamed who drew
  Thy portrait in that thrilling tale of old!
Dead queen, we see thee still, thy beauty cold
As beautiful; thy dauntless heart which knew
No fear, — not even of a king who slew
At pleasure; maiden heart which was not sold,
Though all the maiden flesh the king's red gold
Did buy! The loyal daughter of the Jew,
No hour saw thee forget his misery;
Thou wert not queen until thy race went free;
Yet thoughtful hearts, that ponder slow and deep,
Find doubtful reverence at last for thee;
Thou heldest thy race too dear, thyself too cheap;
Honor no second place for truth can keep.

VASHTI.

N all great Shushan's palaces was there
  Not one, O Vashti, knowing thee so
    well,
Poor uncrowned queen, that he the world could tell
How thou wert pure and loyal-souled as fair?
How it was love which made thee bold to dare
Refuse the shame which madmen would compel?
Not one, who saw the bitter tears that fell
And heard thy cry heart-rending on the air:
"Ah me! My Lord could not this thing have
    meant!
He well might loathe me ever, if I go
Before these drunken princes as a show.
I am his queen: I come of king's descent.
I will not let him bring our crown so low;
He will but bless me when he doth repent!"

BURNT OFFERING.

THE fire leaped up, swift, hot, and red;
    Swift, hot, and red, waiting a prey;
    The woman came with swift, light tread,
  And silently knelt down to lay
Armfuls of leaves upon the fire,
As men lay fagots on a pyre.

Armfuls of leaves which had been bright
    Like painter's tints six months before,
All faded now, a ghastly sight,
    Dusty and colorless, she bore,
And knelt and piled them on the fire,
As men lay fagots on the pyre.

Watching the crackle and the blaze,
    Idly I smiled and idly said:
" Good-by, dead leaves, go dead leaves' ways.
    Next year there will be more as red."
The woman turned, and from the fire
Looked up as from a funeral-pyre.

I saw my idle words had been
    Far crueler than I could know,
And made an old wound bleed again.
  "These are not leaves," she whispered low,
" That I am burning in the fire,
But days, — it is a funeral pyre."

BON VOYAGE.

THERE 'S not an hour but from some sparkling beach
Go joyful men, in fragile ships to sail,
By unknown seas to unknown lands. They hail
The freshening winds with eager hope, and speech
Of wondrous countries which they soon will reach.
Left on the shore, we wave our hands, with pale,
Wet cheeks, but hearts that are ashamed to quail,
Or own the grief which selfishness would teach.
O Death, the fairest lands beyond thy sea
Lie waiting, and thy barks are swift and stanch
And ready. Why do we reluctant launch?
And when our friends their heritage have claimed
Of thee, and entered on it, rich and free,
Oh, why are we of sorrow not ashamed?

NEW YEAR'S MORNING.

ONLY a night from old to new!
   Only a night, and so much wrought!
   The Old Year's heart all weary grew,
But said: "The New Year rest has brought."
The Old Year's heart its hopes laid down,
As in a grave; but, trusting, said:
"The blossoms of the New Year's crown
Bloom from the ashes of the dead."
The Old Year's heart was full of greed;
With selfishness it longed and ached,
And cried: "I have not half I need.
My thirst is bitter and unslaked.
But to the New Year's generous hand
All gifts in plenty shall return;
True loving it shall understand;
By all my failures it shall learn.
I have been reckless; it shall be
Quiet and calm and pure of life.
I was a slave; it shall go free,
And find sweet peace where I leave strife."

NEW YEAR'S MORNING.

Only a night from old to new !
Never a night such changes brought.
The Old Year had its work to do ;
No New Year miracles are wrought.

Always a night from old to new !
Night and the healing balm of sleep !
Each morn is New Year's morn come true,
Morn of a festival to keep.
All nights are sacred nights to make
Confession and resolve and prayer ;
All days are sacred days to wake
New gladness in the sunny air.
Only a night from old to new ;
Only a sleep from night to morn.
The new is but the old come true ;
Each sunrise sees a new year born.

JANUARY.

WINTER! frozen pulse and heart of fire,
What loss is theirs who from thy kingdom
turn
Dismayed, and think thy snow a sculptured urn
Of death! Far sooner in midsummer tire
The streams than under ice. June could not hire
Her roses to forego the strength they learn
In sleeping on thy breast. No fires can burn
The bridges thou dost lay where men desire
In vain to build. O Heart, when Love's sun goes
To northward, and the sounds of singing cease,
Keep warm by inner fires, and rest in peace.
Sleep on content, as sleeps the patient rose.
Walk boldly on the white untrodden snows,
The winter is the winter's own release.

FEBRUARY.

STILL lie the sheltering snows, undimmed
    and white;
  And reigns the winter's pregnant silence
    still;
No sign of spring, save that the catkins fill,
And willow stems grow daily red and bright.
These are the days when ancients held a rite
Of expiation for the old year's ill,
And prayer to purify the new year's will:
Fit days, ere yet the spring rains blur the sight,
Ere yet the bounding blood grows hot with haste,
And dreaming thoughts grow heavy with a greed
The ardent summer's joy to have and taste;
Fit days, to give to last year's losses heed,
To reckon clear the new life's sterner need;
Fit days, for Feast of Expiation placed!

MARCH.

MONTH which the warring ancients strangely styled
  The month of war, — as if in their fierce ways
Were any month of peace ! — in thy rough days
I find no war in Nature, though the wild
Winds clash and clang, and broken boughs are piled
At feet of writhing trees. The violets raise
Their heads without affright, without amaze,
And sleep through all the din, as sleeps a child.
And he who watches well may well discern
Sweet expectation in each living thing.
Like pregnant mother the sweet earth doth yearn ;
In secret joy makes ready for the spring ;
And hidden, sacred, in her breast doth bear
Annunciation lilies for the year.

APRIL.

NO days such honored days as these! While
    yet
    Fair Aphrodite reigned, men seeking wide
For some fair thing which should forever bide
On earth, her beauteous memory to set
In fitting frame that no age could forget,
Her name in lovely April's name did hide,
And leave it there, eternally allied
To all the fairest flowers Spring did beget.
And when fair Aphrodite passed from earth,
Her shrines forgotten and her feasts of mirth,
A holier symbol still in seal and sign,
Sweet April took, of kingdom most divine,
When Christ ascended, in the time of birth
Of spring anemones, in Palestine.

MAY.

MONTH when they who love must love
and wed!
Were one to go to worlds where May is
naught,
And seek to tell the memories he had brought
From earth of thee, what were most fitly said?
I know not if the rosy showers shed
From apple-boughs, or if the soft green wrought
In fields, or if the robin's call be fraught
The most with thy delight. Perhaps they read
Thee best who in the ancient time did say
Thou wert the sacred month unto the old:
No blossom blooms upon thy brightest day
So subtly sweet as memories which unfold
In aged hearts which in thy sunshine lie,
To sun themselves once more before they die.

JUNE.

A MONTH whose promise and fulfilment blend,
And burst in one! it seems the earth can store
In all her roomy house no treasure more;
Of all her wealth no farthing have to spend
On fruit, when once this stintless flowering end.
And yet no tiniest flower shall fall before
It hath made ready at its hidden core
Its tithe of seed, which we may count and tend
Till harvest. Joy of blossomed love, for thee
Seems it no fairer thing can yet have birth?
No room is left for deeper ecstasy?
Watch well if seeds grow strong, to scatter free
Germs for thy future summers on the earth.
A joy which is but joy soon comes to dearth.

JULY.

SOME flowers are withered and some joys
    have died;
The garden reeks with an East Indian
    scent
From beds where gillyflowers stand weak and spent;
The white heat pales the skies from side to side;
But in still lakes and rivers, cool, content,
Like starry blooms on a new firmament,
White lilies float and regally abide.
In vain the cruel skies their hot rays shed;
The lily does not feel their brazen glare.
In vain the pallid clouds refuse to share
Their dews; the lily feels no thirst, no dread.
Unharmed she lifts her queenly face and head;
She drinks of living waters and keeps fair.

AUGUST.

SILENCE again. The glorious symphony
    Hath need of pause and interval of peace.
    Some subtle signal bids all sweet sounds
        cease,
Save hum of insects' aimless industry.
Pathetic summer seeks by blazonry
Of color to conceal her swift decrease.
Weak subterfuge! Each mocking day doth fleece
A blossom, and lay bare her poverty.
Poor middle-agèd summer! Vain this show!
Whole fields of golden-rod cannot offset
One meadow with a single violet;
And well the singing thrush and lily know,
Spite of all artifice which her regret
Can deck in splendid guise, their time to go!

SEPTEMBER.

 GOLDEN month! How high thy gold
is heaped!
The yellow birch-leaves shine like bright
coins strung
On wands; the chestnut's yellow pennons tongue
To every wind its harvest challenge. Steeped
In yellow, still lie fields where wheat was reaped;
And yellow still the corn sheaves, stacked among
The yellow gourds, which from the earth have wrung
Her utmost gold. To highest boughs have leaped
The purple grape, — last thing to ripen, late
By very reason of its precious cost.
O Heart, remember, vintages are lost
If grapes do not for freezing night-dews wait.
Think, while thou sunnest thyself in Joy's estate,
Mayhap thou canst not ripen without frost!

OCTOBER.

THE month of carnival of all the year,
　　When Nature lets the wild earth go its way,
　　And spend whole seasons on a single day.
The spring-time holds her white and purple dear;
October, lavish, flaunts them far and near;
The summer charily her reds doth lay
Like jewels on her costliest array;
October, scornful, burns them on a bier.
The winter hoards his pearls of frost in sign
Of kingdom: whiter pearls than winter knew,
Or Empress wore, in Egypt's ancient line,
October, feasting 'neath her dome of blue,
Drinks at a single draught, slow filtered through
Sunshiny air, as in a tingling wine!

NOVEMBER.

THIS is the treacherous month when autumn days
    With summer's voice come bearing summer's gifts.
Beguiled, the pale down-trodden aster lifts
Her head and blooms again. The soft, warm haze
Makes moist once more the sere and dusty ways,
And, creeping through where dead leaves lie in drifts,
The violet returns. Snow noiseless sifts
Ere night, an icy shroud, which morning's rays
Will idly shine upon and slowly melt,
Too late to bid the violet live again.
The treachery, at last, too late, is plain;
Bare are the places where the sweet flowers dwelt.
What joy sufficient hath November felt?
What profit from the violet's day of pain?

DECEMBER.

THE lakes of ice gleam bluer than the lakes
    Of water 'neath the summer sunshine
        gleamed :
Far fairer than when placidly it streamed,
The brook its frozen architecture makes,
And under bridges white its swift way takes.
Snow comes and goes as messenger who dreamed
Might linger on the road ; or one who deemed
His message hostile gently for their sakes
Who listened might reveal it by degrees.
We gird against the cold of winter wind
Our loins now with mighty bands of sleep,
In longest, darkest nights take rest and ease,
And every shortening day, as shadows creep
O'er the brief noontide, fresh surprises find.

REFRAIN.

OF all the songs which poets sing,
    The ones which are most sweet,
    Are those which at close intervals
    A low refrain repeat;
Some tender word, some syllable,
    Over and over, ever and ever,
While the song lasts,
    Altering never,
Music if sung, music if said,
Subtle like some fine golden thread
    A shuttle casts,
    In and out on a fabric red,
    Till it glows all through
    With the golden hue.
Oh! of all the songs sung,
    No songs are so sweet
As the songs with refrains,
    Which repeat and repeat.

Of all the lives lived,
    No life is so sweet,

As the life where one thought,
  In refrain doth repeat,
Over and over, ever and ever,
  Till the life ends,
  Altering never,
Joy which is felt, but is not said,
Subtler than any golden thread
  Which the shuttle sends
  In and out in a fabric red,
  Till it glows all through
  With a golden hue.
Oh! of all the lives lived,
  Can be no life so sweet
As the life where one thought
  In refrain doth repeat.

"Now name me a thought
  To make life so sweet,
A thought of such joy
  Its refrain to repeat."
Oh! foolish to ask me. Ever, ever
  Who loveth believes,
  But telleth never.
It might be a name, just a name not said,
But in every thought; like a golden thread
  Which the shuttle weaves
  In and out on a fabric red,

REFRAIN.

   Till it glows all through
    With a golden hue.
Oh! of all sweet lives,
   Who can tell how sweet
Is the life which one name
   In refrain doth repeat?

TO AN ABSENT LOVER.

THAT so much change should come when
    thou dost go,
  Is mystery that I cannot ravel quite.
The very house seems dark as when the light
Of lamps goes out. Each wonted thing doth grow
So altered, that I wander to and fro
Bewildered by the most familiar sight,
And feel like one who rouses in the night
From dream of ecstasy, and cannot know
At first if he be sleeping or awake.
My foolish heart so foolish for thy sake
Hath grown, dear one!
                Teach me to be more wise.
I blush for all my foolishness doth lack;
I fear to seem a coward in thine eyes.
Teach me, dear one, — but first thou must
    come back!

CROSSED THREADS.

THE silken threads by viewless spinners
    spun,
    Which float so idly on the summer air,
And help to make each summer morning fair,
Shining like silver in the summer sun,
Are caught by wayward breezes, one by one,
And blown to east and west and fastened there,
Weaving on all the roads their sudden snare.
No sign which road doth safest, freest run,
The wingèd insects know, that soar so gay
To meet their death upon each summer day.
How dare we any human deed arraign;
Attempt to reckon any moment's cost; ,
Or any pathway trust as safe and plain
Because we see not where the threads have crossed?

OUTWARD BOUND.

THE hour has come. Strong hands the anchor raise;
Friends stand and weep along the fading shore,
In sudden fear lest we return no more,
In sudden fancy that he safer stays
Who stays behind; that some new danger lays
New snare in each fresh path untrod before.
Ah, foolish hearts! in fate's mysterious lore
Is written no such choice of plan and days:
Each hour has its own peril and escape;
In most familiar things' familiar shape
New danger comes without or sight or sound;
No sea more foreign rolls than breaks each morn
Across our thresholds when the day is born:
We sail, at sunrise, daily, "outward bound."

SEALED ORDERS.

WHEN ship with "orders sealed" sails out to sea,
   Men eager crowd the wharves, and reverent gaze
Upon their faces whose brave spirits raise
No question if the unknown voyage be
Of deadly peril.   Benedictions free
And prayers and tears are given, and the days
Counted till other ships, on homeward ways,
May bring back message of her destiny.
Yet, all the time, Life's tossing sea is white
With scudding sails which no man reefs or stays
By his own will, for roughest day or night:
Brave, helpless crews, with captain out of sight,
Harbor unknown, voyage of long delays,
They meet no other ships on homeward ways.

TWO.

I.

APART.

ONE place — one roof — one name — their
    daily bread
    In daily sacrament they break
Together, and together take
Perpetual counsel, such as use has fed
The habit of, in words which make
No lie. For courtesy's sweet sake
And pity's, one brave heart whose joy is dead,
Smiles ever, answering words which wake
But weariness ; hides all its ache, —
Its hopeless ache, its longing and its dread ;
Strong as a martyr at the stake
Renouncing self ; striving to slake
The pangs of thirst on bitter hyssop red
With vinegar ! O brave, strong heart !
God sets all days, all hours apart,
Joy cometh at his hour appointed.

II.

TOGETHER.

No touch — no sight — no sound — wide continents
And seas clasp hands to separate
Them from each other now.   Too late !
Triumphant Love has leagued the elements
To do their will.   Hath light a mate
For swiftness?   Can it overweight
The air?   Or doth the sun know accidents?
The light, the air, the sun, inviolate
For them, do constant keep and state
Message of their ineffable contents
And raptures, each in each.   So great
Their bliss of loving, even fate
In parting them, hath found no instruments
Whose bitter pain insatiate
Doth kill it, or their faith abate
In presence of Love's hourly sacraments.

THE GIFT OF GRAPES.

A LEGEND OF THE FOURTH CENTURY.

HE desert sun was sinking red;
   Hot as at noon the light was shed.

Bareheaded, on the scorching sands,
Macarius knelt with claspèd hands,

And prayed, as he had prayed for years,
With smitings and with bitter tears.

"Good hermit, here!" — a hand outstretched, —
It was as if an angel fetched

The purple clusters, dewy blue, —
"Good hermit, here! These grapes for you!"

Swift swept the rider by. The grapes
Lay at the hermit's feet. "Like shapes

"Of magic, sent to tempt my sense,"
Macarius thought. "Sathanas, hence!"

He cried. "I will not touch nor taste.
Yet, were it not wrong such fruit to waste?"

He paused. "I'll leave it at his door,
My neighbor, who with illness sore

"Is like to die. He may partake,
And sin not. Ay, for Jesus' sake,

"I will his dying lips beseech,
Command, as if I were his leech."

Thus speaking, trembling as he spoke,
Such parched desire within him woke,

To taste the grapes, he swiftly ran,
And, kneeling by the dying man,

Held up the clusters, crying, "See,
O brother! these were given me.

"I may not eat them; I am strong;
But thou — it were for thee no wrong.

"Thy fever they will cool, allay;
Thy failing strength revive and stay."

Reproachful turned the dying eyes,
The whispers came like dying sighs:

"Brother, thou mightst do better deed
Than tempt the dying in his need.

"Thy words are but the devil's mesh,
To snare at last my carnal flesh."

Silent, Macarius went his way.
Untouched the purple clusters lay

Beside the dying hermit's bed.
They found them there who found him dead, —

Two brother hermits who each morn,
Water and bread to him had borne.

"He drinks of living waters now,"
They pious said, and smoothed his brow,

And prayed, and laid him in the ground,
Envying the rest he had found.

The purple grapes still lying there,
Filled with sweet scent the desert air.

"Where could these luscious clusters grow?"
"He tasted not," they whispered low;

"But fairer fruit glads now his eyes:
He feasts to-day in paradise."

On each a longing silence fell.
"Brother, they tempt our souls to hell!"

Cried one. The other: "Ay, how weak
Our flesh! Strange that so long we seek

"In vain to dull its carnal sense.
Brother, we'll bear these clusters hence.

"That aged hermit, in the cave,
Perchance these grapes his life might save.

"Thou knowest, but yesterday 't was said
He starves; eats neither pulse nor bread."

Slow braiding baskets, in his door
The aged hermit sat, his store

Of rushes and his water-jar
In reach. He heard their steps afar,

And, as they nearer drew, up-raised
His well-nigh sightless eyes, and gazed

Bewilderedly. "Eat, father, eat!"
The brothers cried, and at his feet,

Rev'rent, the purple clusters laid.
Trembling, but stern, the right hand made

Swift gesture of reproof. " Away ! "
In feeble voice he cried, " and pray

" To be forgiven ! Heinous sin
Is his who lets temptation in."

Meek-bowed, the brothers turned to go.
" Stay ! " said the hermit, whispering low :

" Leave them not here to tempt my sight.
I may not eat. Some other might.

" As each man thinketh in his heart,
So must he reckon duty's part.

" Mayhap some brother, in sore strait,
Even this hour doth sit and wait,

" To whom God sends these clusters sweet
By your pure hands. Be true ! Be fleet ! "

From cave to cave, from cell to cell,
The brothers did their errand well.

In Nitria's desert, hermits then
By scores were dwelling, holy men,

Mistaken saints, who thought to save
Their souls, by making life a grave.

THE GIFT OF GRAPES.

From cave to cave, from cell to cell,
The brothers did their errand well.

At every hermit's feet they laid
The tempting grapes, in vain, nor stayed

Till, at the desert's utmost bound,
Macarius's cell they joyful found, —

Macarius, oldest, holiest saint
Of all the desert. Weary, faint,

They knelt before him. "Father, see
These grapes! they must be meant for thee!

"These many days we bear them now;
And yet they do not withered grow.

"No brother will so much as taste.
'T was Isidore who bade us haste

"To find the man to whom God sent
The luscious gift. They must be meant

"For thee. Thou art the last." "Ay," said
The good Macarius, flushing red

With holy joy, — "Ay; meant for me,
As token of the constancy

"Of all our brothers ! Blessed day
Is this, my brothers ! Go your way !

" Christ fill your souls with lasting peace !
The time is near of my release."

Then, kneeling on the scorching sands,
He stretched toward heaven his claspèd hands,

And prayed, as he had prayed for years,
With smitings and with bitter tears.

Untouched, the grapes lay glowing there,
Filling with scent the desert air.

AVALANCHES.

HEART that on Love's sunny height doth dwell,
And joy unquestioning by day, by night,
Serene in trust because the skies are bright !
Listen to what all Alpine records tell
Of days on which the avalanches fell.
Not days of storm when men were pale with fright,
And watched the hills with anxious, straining sight,
And heard in every sound a note of knell;
But when in heavens still, and blue, and clear,
The sun rode high, — those were the hours to fear.
And so the monks of San Bernard to-day, —
May the Lord count their souls and hold them dear, —
When skies are cloudless, in their convent stay,
And for the souls of dead and dying pray.

A WOMAN'S DEATH-WOUND.

IT left upon her tender flesh no trace.
    The murderer is safe. As swift as light
    The weapon fell, and, in the summer night,
Did scarce the silent, dewy air displace;
'T was but a word. A blow had been less base.
Like dumb beast branded by an iron white
With heat, she turned in blind and helpless flight,
But then remembered, and with piteous face
Came back.   Since then, the world has nothing missed
In her, in voice or smile. But she — each day
She counts until her dying be complete.
One moan she makes, and ever doth repeat:
"O lips that I have loved and kissed and kissed,
Did I deserve to die this bitterest way?"

CHANCE.

THESE things I wondering saw beneath the sun:
That never yet the race was to the swift,
The fight unto the mightiest to lift,
Nor favors unto men whose skill had done
Great works, nor riches ever unto one
Wise man of understanding. All is drift
Of time and chance, and none may stay or sift
Or know the end of that which is begun.
Who waits until the wind shall silent keep,
Will never find the ready hour to sow.
Who watcheth clouds will have no time to reap.
At daydawn plant thy seed, and be not slow
At night. God doth not slumber take nor sleep:
Which seed shall prosper thou canst never know.

SEPTEMBER.

THE golden-rod is yellow;
    The corn is turning brown;
The trees in apple orchards
    With fruit are bending down.

The gentian's bluest fringes
    Are curling in the sun;
In dusty pods the milkweed
    Its hidden silk has spun.

The sedges flaunt their harvest,
    In every meadow nook;
And asters by the brook-side
    Make asters in the brook.

From dewy lanes at morning
    The grapes' sweet odors rise;
At noon the roads all flutter
    With yellow butterflies.

SEPTEMBER.

By all these lovely tokens
   September days are here,
With summer's best of weather,
   And autumn's best of cheer.

But none of all this beauty
   Which floods the earth and air
Is unto me the secret
   Which makes September fair.

'T is a thing which I remember;
   To name it thrills me yet:
One day of one September
   I never can forget.

APPEAL.

" LOVE, whom I so love, in this sore strait
Of thine, fall not! Below thy very feet
I kneel, so much I reverence thee, so sweet
It is to every pulse of mine to wait
Thy lightest pleasure, and to bind my fate
To thine by humblest service. Incomplete
All heaven, Love, if there thou dost not greet
Me, with perpetual need which I can sate,
I and no other! So I dare to pray
To thee this prayer. It is not wholly prayer.
The solemn worships of the ages lay
Even on God a solemn bond. I dare, —
Thy worshipper, thy lowly, loving mate, —
I dare to say, O Love, thou must be great!"

WRECK.

[By the laws of the Rhodians divers were allowed a share of the wreck in proportion to the depth to which they had gone in search of it.]

O many fathoms deep my sweet ship lies,
    No ripple marks the place. The gulls'
        white wings
Pause not; the boatman idly sleeps or sings,
Floating above; and smile to smile, with skies
That bend and shine, the sunny water vies.
Too heavy freight, and of too costly things,
My sweet ship bore. No tempest's mutterings
Warned me; but in clear noon, before my eyes
She sudden faltered, rocked, and with each sail
Full set, went down!
                O Heart! in diver's mail
Wrap thee. Breathe not till, standing on her deck,
Thou has confronted all thy loss and wreck.
Poor coward Heart! — thou darest not plunge? —
    For thee
There lies no other pearl in any sea.

THE HEART OF A ROSE.

ROSE like a hollow cup with a brim, —
   A brim as pink as the after-glow;
   Deep down in its heart gold stamens swim,
   Tremble and swim in a sea of snow.
My Love set it safe in a crystal glass,
Gently as petals float down at noon.
Low, in a whisper, my Love's voice said:
"Look quick! In an hour it will be dead.
I picked it because it will die so soon.
Now listen, dear Heart, as the seconds pass,
What the rose will say," my Love's voice said.

I look and I listen. The flushed pink brim
Is still as June's warmest after-glow;
Silent as stars the gold stamens swim,
Tremble and swim in their sea of snow.
I dare not breathe on the crystal glass,
Lest one sweet petal should fall too soon.
False was the whisper my Love's voice said, —
If he had not picked it, it had been dead;
But now it will live an eternal noon,
And I shall hear as the seconds pass
What the rose will say till I am dead.

ACQUAINTED WITH GRIEF.

DOST know Grief well? Hast known her long?
  So long, that not with gift or smile,
Or gliding footstep in the throng,
  She can deceive thee by her guile?

So long, that with unflinching eyes
  Thou smilest to thyself apart,
To watch each flimsy, fresh disguise
  She plans to stab anew thy heart?

So long, thou barrest up no door
  To stay the coming of her feet?
So long, thou answerest no more,
  Lest in her ear thy cry be sweet?

Dost know the voice in which she says,
  " No more henceforth our paths divide;
In loneliest nights, in crowded days,
  I am forever by thy side"?

Then dost thou know, perchance, the spell
  The gods laid on her at her birth, —
The viewless gods who mingle well
  Strange love and hate of us on earth.

Weapon and time, the hour, the place,
  All these are hers to take, to choose,
To give us neither rest nor grace,
  Not one heart-throb to miss or lose.

All these are hers; yet stands she, slave,
  Helpless before our one behest:
The gods, that we be shamed not, gave,
  And locked the secret in our breast.

She to the gazing world must bear
  Our crowns of triumph, if we bid;
Loyal and mute, our colors wear,
  Sign of her own forever hid.

Smile to our smile, song to our song,
  With songs and smiles our roses fling,
Till men turn round in every throng,
  To note such joyous pleasuring,

And ask, next morn, with eyes that lend
  A fervor to the words they say,
" What is her name, that radiant friend
  Who walked beside you yesterday?"

FEALTY.

THE thing I count and hold as fealty —
The only fealty to give or take —
Doth never reckoning keep, and coldly make
Bond to itself with this or that to be
Content as wage ; the wage unpaid, to free
Its hand from service, and its love forsake,
Its faith cast off, as one from dreams might wake
At morn, and smiling watch the vision flee.
Such fealty is treason in disguise.
Who trusts it, his death-warrant sealed doth bear.
Love looks at it with angry, wondering eyes ;
Love knows the face true fealty doth wear,
The pulse that beats unchanged by alien air,
Or hurts, or crimes, until the loved one dies.

VISION.

BY subtile secrets of discovered law
    Men well have measured the horizon's round,
    Kept record of the speed of light and sound,
Have close defined by reasoning without flaw
The utmost human vision ever saw
Unaided, and have arrant sought and found
Devices countless to extend its bound.
Bootless their secrets all! My eyes but stray
To eastward, and majestic, bright, arise
Peaks of a range which three days distant lies!
And of the faces, too, that light my day
Most clear, one is a continent away,
The other shines above the farthest skies!

THE POET'S FORGE.

HE lies on his back, the idling smith,
    A lazy, dreaming fellow is he ;
    The sky is blue, or the sky is gray,
He lies on his back the livelong day,
Not a tool in sight ; say what they may,
    A curious sort of a smith is he.

The powers of the air are in league with him ;
    The country around believes it well ;
The wondering folk draw spying near ;
Never sight nor sound do they see or hear ;
No wonder they feel a little fear ;
    When is it his work is done so well?

Never sight nor sound to see or hear ;
    The powers of the air are in league with him ;
High over his head his metals swing,
Fine gold and silver to shame the king ;
We might distinguish their glittering,
    If once we could get in league with him.

High over his head his metals swing;
   He hammers them idly year by year,
Hammers and chuckles a low refrain:
" A bench and book are a ball and chain,
The adze is better tool than the plane;
   What's the odds between now and next year?"

Hammers and chuckles his low refrain,
   A lazy, dreaming fellow is he:
When sudden, some day, his bells peal out,
And men, at the sound, for gladness shout;
He laughs and asks what it's all about;
   Oh, a curious sort of smith is he!

VANITY OF VANITIES.

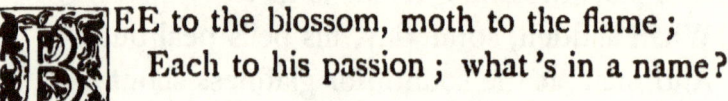EE to the blossom, moth to the flame;
   Each to his passion; what's in a name?

Red clover's sweetest, well the bee knows;
No bee can suck it; lonely it blows.

Deep lies its honey, out of reach, deep;
What use in honey hidden to keep?

Robbed in the autumn, starving for bread;
Who stops to pity a honey-bee dead?

Star-flames are brightest, blazing the skies;
Only a hand's-breadth the moth-wing flies.

Fooled with a candle, scorched with a breath;
Poor little miller, a tawdry death!

Life is a honey, life is a flame;
Each to his passion; what's in a name?

VANITY OF VANITIES.

Swinging and circling, face to the sun,
Brief little planet, how it doth run !

Bee-time and moth-time, add the amount ;
White heat and honey, who keeps the count ?

Gone some fine evening, a spark out-tost !
The world no darker for one star lost !

Bee to the blossom, moth to the flame ;
Each to his passion ; what's in a name ?

MORN.

N what a strange bewilderment do we
    Awake each morn from out the brief
    night's sleep.
Our struggling consciousness doth grope and
    creep
Its slow way back, as if it could not free
Itself from bonds unseen. Then Memory,
Like sudden light, outflashes from its deep
The joy or grief which it had last to keep
For us; and by the joy or grief we see
The new day dawneth like the yesterday;
We are unchanged; our life the same we knew
Before. I wonder if this is the way
We wake from death's short sleep, to struggle
    through
A brief bewilderment, and in dismay
Behold our life unto our old life true.

QUATRAINS.

THE MONEY-SEEKER.

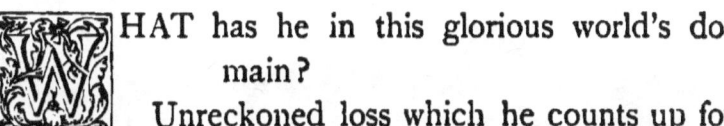HAT has he in this glorious world's domain?
Unreckoned loss which he counts up for gain,
Unreckoned shame, of which he feels no stain,
Unreckoned dead he does not know were slain.

What things does he take with him when he dies?
Nothing of all that he on earth did prize:
Unto his grovelling feet and sordid eyes
How difficult and empty seem the skies!

THE LOVER.

He knows the utmost secret of the earth:
The golden sunrise's and sunset's worth;
The pregnancy of every blossom's birth;
The hidden name of every creature's mirth.

He knows all measures of the pulse's beat;
He knows all pathless paths of human feet;
He knows what angels know not of the sweet
Fulfilments when love's being is complete.

He knows all deadly soils where poisons bloom;
He knows the fated road where joy makes room
For nameless terrors and eternal gloom:
God help him in his sad omniscient doom!

RELEASE.

F one had watched a prisoner many a year,
    Standing behind a barrèd window-pane,
    Fettered with heavy handcuff and with
        chain,
And gazing on the blue sky, far and clear;
And suddenly some morning he should hear
The man had in the night contrived to gain
His freedom and was safe, would this bring pain?
Ah! would it not to dullest heart appear
Good tidings?
           Yesterday I looked on one
Who lay as if asleep in perfect peace.
His long imprisonment for life was done.
Eternity's great freedom his release
Had brought. Yet they who loved him called him
        dead,
And wept, refusing to be comforted.

WHERE?

MY snowy eupatorium has dropped
    Its silver threads of petals in the night;
    No signal told its blossoming had stopped;
Its seed-films flutter silent, ghostly white:
    No answer stirs the shining air,
      As I ask, "Where?"

Beneath the glossy leaves of winter-green
Dead lily-bells lie low, and in their place
A rounded disk of pearly pink is seen,
Which tells not of the lily's fragrant grace:
    No answer stirs the shining air,
      As I ask, "Where?"

This morning's sunrise does not show to me
Seed-film or fruit of my sweet yesterday;
Like falling flowers, to realms I cannot see
Its moments floated silently away:
    No answer stirs the shining air,
      As I ask, "Where?"

EMIGRAVIT.

ITH sails full set, the ship her anchor weighs.
    Strange names shine out beneath her figure
        head.
What glad farewells with eager eyes are said!
What cheer for him who goes, and him who stays!
Fair skies, rich lands, new homes, and untried days
Some go to seek; the rest but wait instead
Until the next stanch ship her flag doth raise.
Who knows what myriad colonies there are
Of fairest fields, and rich, undreamed-of gains
Thick planted in the distant shining plains
Which we call sky because they lie so far?
Oh, write of me, not "Died in bitter pains,"
But "Emigrated to another star!"

MY TENANTS.

NEVER had a title-deed
To my estate. But little heed
Eyes give to me, when I walk by
My fields, to see who occupy.
Some clumsy men who lease and hire
And cut my trees to feed their fire,
Own all the land that I possess,
And tax my tenants to distress.
And if I said I had been first,
And, reaping, left for them the worst,
That they were beggars at the hands
Of dwellers on my royal lands,
With idle laugh of passing scorn
As unto words of madness born,
They would reply.
     I do not care ;
They cannot crowd the charmèd air ;
They cannot touch the bonds I hold
On all that they have bought and sold.
They can waylay my faithful bees,
Who, lulled to sleep, with fatal ease,

Are robbed. Is one day's honey sweet
Thus snatched? All summer round my feet
In golden drifts from plumy wings,
In shining drops on fragrant things,
Free gift, it came to me. My corn,
With burnished banners, morn by morn,
Comes out to meet and honor me;
The glittering ranks spread royally
Far as I walk. When hasty greed
Tramples it down for food and seed,
I, with a certain veiled delight,
Hear half the crop is lost by blight.

   Letter of law these may fulfil,
Plant where they like, slay what they will,
Count up their gains and make them great;
Nevertheless, the whole estate
Always belongs to me and mine.
We are the only royal line.
And though I have no title-deed
My tenants pay me loyal heed
When our sweet fields I wander by
To see what strangers occupy.

THE STORY OF BOON.[1]

It haunts my thoughts morn, night, and
    noon,
The story of the woman, Boon, —
Haunts me like restless ghost, until
I give myself to do its will ;
Cries voiceless, yet as voices cry, —
"O singer, can this tale pass by
Untold by thee ? Thy heart is wrung
In vain, if dies the song unsung."
I am unworthy : master hands
Should strike the chords, and fill the lands
From sea to sea with melody
All reverent, yet with harmony
Majestic, jubilant, to tell
How love must love, if love loves well ;
How once incarnate love was found
On earth, dishonored, martyr-crowned,
Crowned by a heathen woman's name, —
O blessed Boon, of peerless fame !

[1] This story of Boon is strictly true. It is told by Mrs. Leonowens, the English Governess at the Siamese court. She took it down from Choy's own lips.

In Siam's court the Buddhist King
Held festival. Fair girls to sing,
And dance, and play, were led between
Close ranks of Amazons in green
And gold. In chariot milk-white
Of ivory, and glittering bright
With flowers garlanded, rode Choy,
The young, the beautiful; with joy
And subtle pride no words could tell,
Her virgin bosom rose and fell.
No dream the Siam maiden knew
More high or blest than that which grew
In Choy's poor blinded heart, — to be
The favorite of the King, and see
The other wives beneath her feet.
From babyhood, that this was sweet
The child was taught. How should she know
They told her false, and worked her woe!

The song, the dance, the play, were done,
Choy's fatal triumph had been won.
The old king's bleared and lustful eyes
Had marked her for his next new prize.
Asking her name, as low she bowed
Before the throne, he called aloud, —
"Which of my nobles springs to lead
Her chariot ponies? Do I need
Speak farther?"
    On the instant, two
Young nobles robed in white sprang through

The crowd, and kneeling as to queen,
With low-bent head and reverent mien,
They walked the chariot beside.
The bands burst forth in swelling tide
Of music, and the curtain fell.
One noble, smitten by the spell
Of Choy's great beauty, whispered, "God,
How beautiful thou art!"
              "My Lord,
Have care," the scornful Choy exclaimed:
"'T were ill for thee, if thou wert blamed
By me."
        The other noble silent gazed,
With eyes whose glance strange tumult raised
Within Choy's breast. He did not speak:
All spoken words had fallen weak,
After his look. Yet Choy's heart burned
To hear his voice. Sudden she turned,
And leaning forward said, "How now,
What seest thou in air that thou
Art dumb?"
          With trembling lips he spoke, —
"O Lady, till thy sweet voice broke
Upon the air, I thought I saw
An angel; now, with no less awe,
But greater joy, I see thou art
A woman."
         Ah, they know not heart

Of man or woman, who declare
That love needs time to love and dare.
His altars wait, — not day nor name,
Only the touch of sacred flame.

The song, the dance, the play were done.
Oh, fatal triumph Choy had won!
Oh, hateful life she thought was sweet!
She knelt before the old king's feet,
A slave, a toy, a purchased thing,
Which to his worn-out sense might bring
Pleasure again of touch, of sight.
Doting, he named her " Chorm," " Delight,"
Decked her with jewels, gave her power,
And day and night, and hour by hour,
With hideous caresses sought
Joy in the thing which he had bought.
And hour by hour, and night and day,
Wasted poor Choy's young life away.
One thrilling voice, one glowing face,
One thought of such a love's embrace,
Haunted her thoughts, and racked her breast,
Robbed her of peace, robbed her of rest,
Made of her life such living lie,
Such torture, she but prayed to die.

Months passed, and she knew not the name
Of him she loved. At last there came

The fated day. A woman slave,
New in the palace, quickly gave,
Answering Choy's artful questioning,
The noble's name.
     "Ah, go and bring
Me news of him," said Choy. "He bore
Himself so loftily, I more
Recall him than all else that day.
Seek out minutely in what way
He lives; what may his harem hold.
He seemed to me so silent, cold,
No doubt some Houri keeps him chained,"
With scornful laugh, but poorly feigned,
Cried Choy.
   At dusk of night returned
The slave, with wondrous tale, which burned
Itself on Choy's glad heart.
      The Duke,
Phaya Phi Chitt his name, forsook
His harem on the day he led
The Favorite's chariot ponies. Dead
He seemed to all he once had loved:
No fear, no joy, his spirit moved.
His friends believed that he was mad,
Or else some mortal illness had.
A feverish joy filled all Choy's thought,
She knew by what this change was wrought.
Love's keenest pain, if shared like this,
No longer seemed a pain, but bliss.

Again the faithful slave she sent,
With message of one word, which meant
But " I remember."
                              " I love much,"
The Duke sent back. Ah, madness such
As this was never seen. The halls
Of tyrants' palaces have walls
Higher than Love's and Hope's last breath,
Wider than Life, deeper than Death!

Embroidered with a thread of gold
On silk, and hidden fold on fold,
As if an amulet she wore,
Her lover's name the poor Choy bore
By night, by day, upon her heart.
The new slave woman, with an art
As tender as a sister's, sought
To comfort her. Each day she brought
New message from the Duke, each night
Lay at her mistress' feet till light.
O Buddha! pitiful, divine,
All-seeing, gav'st thou no sign
To warn these faithful, loving three,
Who were as faithful unto thee
As to each other! Didst thou teach
The cruel tyrant how to reach
Their life blood, that thy arm might save
Them by the surety of the grave?

Might give to their expiring breath
The gift of life, in shape of death?
Ah, Buddha! pitiful, divine,
Thy gifts of death record no sign
Of life beyond.   Our weak hearts crave
Some voice of surety for the grave.

The hours grew ripe: the hour was set,
The night had come.   Choy slumbered yet,
While faithful Boon, with footsteps light,
Made all things ready for their flight.
Sudden a clash of arms, — a gleam
Of fire of torches!   From her dream
Choy waked, and on her threshold saw,
Dread sight which chilled her blood with awe,
Standing with panting voice and breath,
Maï Taïe, Mother of Death,
Cruelest of all the Amazons,
Slayer of all convicted ones
Who braved the tyrant's wrath and hate.
Choy called on Boon.   Too late! too late!
Boon fettered lay with gag and chain;
Most piteous eyes, faithful in pain,
Unto her mistress lifting still.
With blows and jeers wreaking their will,
The soldier women, fierce and strong,
Dragged weeping Choy and Boon along
The by-ways of the silent town,
And flung them, chained and helpless, down

Into a dark and loathsome cell.
Soon as their footsteps' echoes fell
Faintly afar, Choy whispered low, —
"O Boon, dear Boon! tell me hast thou
Confessed?"

"Dear Lady, no!" she cried.
" No tortures tyrants ever tried
Shall wring from me one word of blame
Against Phaya Phi Chitt's dear name."
That instant, flashing through Choy's heart
Strange instinct swept.

"Tell me who art
Thou, Boon," she said: "why dost thou cling
To me through all this suffering?
All other women I have known
Had left me now to die alone.
O Boon, conceal from me no more!
Tell me the truth in this dread hour!"
Then, looking newly at her face,
She saw it beauty had, and grace;
Saw that the feet were lithe and fine,
The hands were small and smooth: each sign
Of tender nurture and high blood
This loving woman bore, who stood
To her as slave. Unearthly sweet
Grew Boon's pale face, as to the feet
Of Choy, all crippled, chained, she crept,
And, as she strove to speak, but wept

And sobbed, —
             "O Lady dear, forgive
That I deceived thee! I but live
For thy dear Duke. I am his wife!"
Dumb wonder sealed Choy's lips. A strife
Of fierce mistrust warred in her breast.
At last, stern-faced, "Tell me the rest,"
She said.
             Closer, more humbly still
Boon crept, and said, —
                       "Lady, I will;
And, by the heart of Buddha, thou
Canst but forgive when thou dost know
The whole.
           "The day my husband came
Home from the fête, he spoke thy name
And told thy beauty unto me,
And said that from that moment he,
His thought, his heart, his blood, were thine, —
Thine utterly, and no more mine
Again. What could I do but weep?
I saw him pine. No food, no sleep,
He took. I thought that he must die.
What could I do? O Lady, I
So loved him that I longed as he
That fate might give him joy and thee.
I vowed to him that I would win
Thee for his wife. How to begin

I knew not, when I found thou wert
The King's last favorite.   It hurt
My pride to be a slave.   The gold
Lies in the sea for which I sold
Myself to thee, rather than break
My vow.   But easy for his sake,
I loved him so, thy service came,
Soon as I found that his dear name
Was dear to thee as thine to him ;
That, when I spoke it, it could dim
Thine eyes with passion's tears, like those
Which he had shed in passion's throes,
For want of thee.   O Lady, none
Of all thy sighs and tears, not one,
But I have flown and faithful told,
That he might know thou wert not cold.
Each word of beauty, nobleness,
Which thou didst speak, I bore to bless
His heart with knowledge more complete
Of thee.   O Lady, the deceit
Was only for his precious sake
And thine : no other way to take
I knew.   My husband is so great,
So good, I was but humble mate
For him.   As shadow follows shape,
My heart in life cannot escape
From following his ; nor yet in death
Shall it be changed : with dying breath,

From Buddha I one joy will wrest,
That he find rapture in thy breast."
Boon ceased, and in her slender hands,
Which scarce could lift her fetter bands,
Buried her face.   Choy did not speak.
Her reverence knew not where to seek
For fitting words which she might dare
To use to Boon.   The midnight air
Heard only sobs, as close between
Her arms she drew Boon's head to lean
Upon her breast.   The long night waned,
And still in silence sat the chained
And helpless women.   Strange thoughts filled
The heart of Choy.   Her love seemed chilled,
Poor, and untrue, beside this one
Great deed she never could have done.
"Ah, me! his wife has loved him best,"
In bitterness her heart confessed,
Yet jealousy for shame was dead.
Her tears fell loving on Boon's head:
"Dear Boon," she whispered soft and low,
"To Buddha pitiful we go."

Next morning when the judges dread
Cross-questioned Boon, she simply said,
"My Lords, what can a poor slave know?"
Weary at last, the fearful blow
Of lashes on her naked feet
They ordered.   Blood ran down the sweet

Soft flesh : still came the answer low,
"My Lords, what can a poor slave know?
Be pitiful!" The swift blows fell
Again : no cry, no sound, to tell
That it was pain, Boon gave ; no sign
Of faltering. They poured down wine
To stay her strength, and then again, —
Oh, surely fiends they were, not men! —
Again, from slender neck to waist,
The cutting blows in angry haste
With tenfold violence they laid.
Each blow a line of red blood made ;
Yet, when they paused, the answer came
Steadfast, heroic, in the same
Pathetic words, more feeble, slow,
"My Lords, what can a poor slave know?"
Then in the torture of the screw,
Whose pain has led strong men to do
Dishonor to their souls and God,
They bound this woman's hands. Sweat stood
In bloody drops along her brow,
Yet from her lips not even now
Was heard one syllable.
     In rage,
The baffled tyrants to assuage
Her sufferings tried every art
Which could be tried by kindest heart,
And snatched her back from death again,
Again to tortures fresh ; in vain !

Night came, and from her lips no word
Had fallen. All night they faintly stirred,
As if in sleep she dreamed and spoke.
Choy watching, weeping by her, took
Her hand, and said, —
      "Oh, tell thy Choy,
Art thou in mortal pain?"
       "My joy
Is greater than my pain," she said,
"That this poor flesh hath not betrayed
My love. Thanking great Buddha now,
I pray unceasing, till we go
Again to torture." Then no more
Boon spoke. To Choy, but little lower
Than angel she appeared. Ah! true
It was the wife loved best! Love knew
His own. His angels comforted
Her soul with joy through hours which bred
But anguish in Choy's breast.
       Too soon
Came cruel day, and brought to Boon
Again the lash, the screw; again
Unto the door of death in vain
They tortured her: no word escaped
Her bloodless lips. Her face seemed shaped
Of iron, so calm, so resolute;
A superhuman light her mute
And upward gaze transfigured, till
In awe the torturers stood still.

Then, binding up her wounds, they laid
Her on a couch to rest. New shade
Of anguish now her face revealed,
Waiting Choy's words. All unconcealed,
No doubt, the weaker love lay bare
Before her instinct. It could dare
For self: now that for self remained
No hope, no future to be gained,
Could it for him be true, be great?
Ah, this true torture was, — to wait
Another woman's courage! Eyes
Of fire Boon fixed on Choy. To rise
She helpless strove, in impulse vain,
As if by touch she could sustain
Choy's strength. Her gaze was like a cry.
"Oh, what is death, is suffering, by
The side of truth? If thou dost love
Another, thought of self can move
Thee not. If thou dost love, to bear
The worst is nothing. Dost thou dare
Betray, thou art a coward, liar!"
Entreated, warned Boon's eyes of fire.
They held Choy's eyes as by a spell.
Feeble the judges' stern tones fell,
Idle the threats of torture seemed,
Beside the scorching look which gleamed
Upon that woman's face. Thus stayed
And stung, Choy bore the blows which laid

Her quivering flesh in furrows. Feet
And neck and shoulders, all the sweet
Fair skin was torn: her blood ran down
As Boon's had run, — not of her own
Resolve, but born of Boon's the strength
Which silent sealed her lips. At length
The one sure pain which torturers know
They tried. No rack, no fire, no blow,
Is dreadful as the screw. At first
Sharp turn it gave, a loud cry burst
From Choy, —

"O Boon, forgive, forgive!
I cannot bear this pain, and live!"
And, shrieking out her lover's name,
She cowered before Boon's eyes of flame.
One cry of uttermost despair
From Boon rang out upon the air,
Her fettered arms above her head
She lifted, and fell back as dead.
Ah! true it was, the wife loved best!
How true, that cry of Choy's confessed.
To love which she had so betrayed,
No prayer she for forgiveness made:
On him whom she had thought her life
She called not, but upon his wife.

Swift sped the feet of them who sought
The lover. Ere the noon, they brought

Him also. Boon, with anguished eyes,
Beheld him there. She could not rise,
But, creeping on her hands and feet,
She cried, in tones unearthly sweet, —
"O Lords! O Judges! look at me,
And listen. It was I, not he.
I am his wife. I laid the plot.
Except for me, the thought had not
Been his. 'T was only I deceived
The Lady Choy. He but believed
What I desired. The guilt is mine,
All mine. Tell them it was not thine,
My husband, — I can bear the whole."
And, as she turned to him, the soul
Of love ineffable set smile
Upon her face. Her piteous guile,
Transparent, thrilled each heart and ear
That heard her pleading voice. A tear
Fell from the sternest Amazon,
Fierce Khoon Thow App, as in a tone
No mortal from her lips had heard
Before, she said, "O Boon, what stirred
Thy heart to this? Thy motive tell!"
The question all unanswered fell.
Boon lay again as if in death,
With closèd eyes and gasping breath.

All night, low on the dark cell's floor,
Lay Boon and Choy; for Boon no more

Remained in life. When Choy crept near,
And humbly spoke, she answered, "Dear,
Farewell!"—no other word. Choy strove,—
Poor Choy! her feebler, lesser love
Avenging on herself its sin,—
Strove from the greater love to win
Some healing stay. Too sweet to pain,
Too loyal and too true to feign,
Boon made but one reply, which fell
Fainter and fainter, "Dear, farewell!"

That night, at midnight, sat the King
And Lords in council. For the thing
Phaya Phi Chitt and Choy had planned,
Scarcely in all that cruel land
Was known a punishment which seemed
Sufficient. Fierce his red wrath gleamed,
As cried the King,—
                    "At dawn shall fly
The vultures with their hungry cry.
Rare feast for them ready by noon
Shall be: three traitors' bodies hewn
In pieces, and with offal cast
Abroad, that to the very last
Low grade of life they may return,
And grovel with the beasts to learn,
Through countless ages, in what way
Kings punish when their slaves betray.

Long generations shall forget
Their base-born names, ere souls are set
Again within their foul, false flesh,
To murder love and trust afresh!"[1]

Ah! true it was, the wife loved best!
Love knew his own, gave her his rest;
And, to the other woman, doom
Of life-long woe and life-long gloom.
O cruel friends who prayed the King,
Who dreamed Choy to this world could cling!
Reprieved from death, to life condemned,
Sad prisoner forever hemmed
Within the hated palace-wall;
By all despised, and shunned by all,
Lonely and broken-hearted, she
Weeps day and night in misery.
And day and night one picture haunts
Her weary brain, her sorrow taunts, —
Picture of Buddha's fairest fields,
Where every hour new transport yields,
And where the lover whom she slew,
Loyal at last, and glad and true,
In full Elysium's perfect rest,
Walks with the one who loved him best!

---

[1] The Siamese believe that, whenever a dead body is not burned, its soul is condemned to begin life again in the lowest animal form.

It haunts me morn, and night, and noon:
This story of the woman, Boon,—
Haunts me like restless ghost, that says,—
"Oh, where is love in these sad days!
Rise up, and in my might and name
Plead for the altar and the flame."
I am unworthy: master hands
Should strike the chords, and fill the lands
From sea to sea with melody
Of such transcendent harmony
That it all jubilant might tell
How love must love, if love loves well.
Yet, telling all, and flooding lands
With melody, the master hands
Could strike no deeper chord than I,
When from a woman's heart I cry,—
"O martyred Boon, of peerless fame,
Incarnate in thy life, Love came!"

THE VICTORY OF PATIENCE.

ARMED of the gods! Divinest conqueror!
   What soundless hosts are thine! Nor
      pomp, nor state,
Nor token, to betray where thou dost wait.
All Nature stands, for thee, ambassador;
Her forces all thy serfs, for peace or war.
Greatest and least alike, thou rul'st their fate, —
The avalanche chained until its century's date,
The mulberry leaf made robe for emperor!
Shall man alone thy law deny? — refuse
Thy healing for his blunders and his sins?
Oh, make us thine! Teach us who waits best sues;
Who longest waits of all most surely wins.
When Time is spent, Eternity begins.
To doubt, to chafe, to haste, doth God accuse.

GOD'S LIGHT-HOUSES.

HEN night falls on the earth, the sea
    From east to west lies twinkling bright
With shining beams from beacons high
    Which flash afar a friendly light.

The sailor's eyes, like eyes in prayer,
    Turn unto them for guiding ray:
If storms obscure their radiance,
    The great ships helpless grope their way.

When night falls on the earth, the sky
    Looks like a wide, a boundless main.
Who knows what voyagers sail there?
    Who names the ports they seek and gain?

Are not the stars like beacons set
    To guide the argosies that go
From universe to universe,
    Our little world above, below? —

On their great errands solemn bent,
   In their vast journeys unaware
Of our small planet's name or place
   Revolving in the lower air.

O thought too vast! O thought too glad!
   An awe most rapturous it stirs.
From world to world God's beacons shine:
   God means to save his mariners!

SONGS OF BATTLE.

OLD as the world — no other things so old;
    Nay, older than the world, else, how had sprung
    Such lusty strength in them when earth was young? —
Stand valor and its passion hot and bold,
Insatiate of battle. How, else, told
Blind men, born blind, that red was fitting tongue
Mute, eloquent, to show how trumpets rung
When armies charged and battle-flags unrolled?
Who sings of valor speaks for life, for death,
Beyond all death, and long as life is life,
In rippled waves the eternal air his breath
Eternal bears to stir all noble strife.
Dead Homer from his lost and vanished grave
Keeps battle glorious still and soldiers brave.

NO MAN'S LAND.

WHO called it so? What accident
    The wary phase devised?
What wandering fancy thither went,
    And lingered there surprised?

Ah, no man's land! O sweet estate
    Illimitably fair!
No measure, wall, or bar or gate.
    Secure as sky or air.

No greed, no gain; not sold or bought,
    Unmarred by name or brand,
Not dreamed of or desired or sought,
    Nor visioned, "no man's land."

Suns set and rise, and rise and set,
    Whole summers come and go;
And winters pay the summer's debt,
    And years of west wind blow;

And harvests of wild seed-times fill,
   And seed and fill again;
And blossoms bloom at blossoms' will,
   By blossoms overlain;

And day and night, and night and day,
   Uncounted suns and moons,
By silent shadows mark and stay
   Unreckoned nights and noons:

Ah, "no man's land," hast thou a lover,
   Thy wild, sweet charm who sees?
The stars look down; the birds fly over;
   Art thou alone with these?

Ah, "no man's land," when died thy lover,
   Who left no trace to tell?
Thy secret we shall not discover;
   The centuries keep it well!

JUST OUT OF SIGHT.

I.

N idle reverie, one winter's day,
I watched the narrow vista of a street,
Where crowds of men with noisy, hurry-
 ing feet
And eager eyes went on their restless way.
Idly I noted where the boundary lay,
At which the distance did my vision cheat,
Past which each figure fading fast did fleet,
And seem to meet and vanish in the gray.
Sudden there came to me a thought, oft told,
But newly shining then like flash of light, —
"This death, the dread of which turns us so cold,
Outside of our own fears has no stronghold;
'T is but a boundary, past which, in white,
Our friends are walking still, just out of sight!"

II.

"Just out of sight!" Ay, truly, that is all!
Take comfort in the words, and be deceived
All ye who can, or have not been bereaved!
"Just out of sight." 'T is easy to recall

A face, a voice. O foolish words, and small
And bitter cheer! Men have all this believed,
And yet, in agony, to death have grieved,
For one " just out of sight," beneath a pall!
" Just out of sight." It means the whole of woe :
One sudden stricken blind who loved the light ;
One starved where he had feasted day and night ;
One who was crowned, to beggary brought low ;
All this death doeth, going to and fro
And putting those we love " just out of sight."

SEPTEMBER WOODS.

GIRT round by meadows wearing shabby
    weeds
  For clover's early death, and sentried by
  The tireless locust, with his muffled click
Of secret weapon, at each footfall, stand
The woods.
          September, smiling treacherous smiles,
And bearing in his hand a hollow truce
Which gentle Summer trusts, can enter free.
O fatal trust! Her sacred inner court
Of Holies, holiest, the lovely queen
Throws open to the ally of her foe.
By day, with sunny look and gracious air
He wins her heart and wears her colors. Night
Beholds him, in his white and gleaming mail,
Alert and noiseless, following the dews,
Her faithful messengers, waylaying them
With sudden cruel death, and, in their stead,
His own foul treason bearing through the realm.
Lured by his guile, the green and twining vines
Array themselves in party-colored robes
And loosely flaunt, unknowing 't is their death.

The low Bunch-Berry her nun's white lays by,
And wearing claret satin, decks her breast
With knots of scarlet beads.   This sin, O sweet,
In resurrection of the coming Spring,
Shall be forgiven thee, and thou again
Shalt rise, as white as snow.
       The fragrant ferns,
And clinging mosses, to whom Summer kind
Had been, more than to other lowly things,
Are true; and not till they are trampled low
By icy warriors, will they refuse
Their emerald carpet to her tread, and then,
In cold white grief, will die around her feet:
The simpering Birch, unstable in the wind,
Is first to break his faith, and cheaply bought
By gold, in brazen vanity, lifts up
His arms, and broadly waves the glittering price
Of his dishonor: Poplars next and Elms
Grow envious of the yellow show, and hold
Their hands for traitor's wages; but more scant
And dim the golden tokens gained by them;
For now disloyalty has spread, and grown
More bold of front: whole clans are cheaply won.
In hostile signal fires from hill to hill,
The Maples blaze; the tangling Sumach-trees
Of glowing spikes build crimson ladders up
The wall; ungainly Moosewood strives and creeps
And shakes his purple-spotted banner out
Defiantly; the sturdy Beeches throw

Their harvest down, and bristle in a suit
Of leathern points: all is revolt, and all
Is lost for Summer!
                    Vainly now she showers
By brook and pool her white and purple stars,
And lifts in all the fields her Golden-Rod;
In vain thin scarlet streamers sets along
The meadows, and to Gentian's pallid lips
Of blue calls back the chilled and torpid bee;
Sweet queen, her kingdom rocks! Her only stay
And comfort now, the loving Pines who wait
In solemn grief, unmoved and undismayed
By guile or threats, and to their farthest kin,
A haughty and untarnished race, will keep
Eternally inviolate and green
Their sworn allegiance to her and all
Her name! Encircled by their arms she dies;
And not the deadliest thrusts of wintry spears,
Nor sweeping avalanche of snow and ice,
Can daunt them from their silent watch around
Her sepulchre, nor from their faithful hold
Can wrest the babe, who, hid in sacred depths
And fed on sacred food, and nurtured till
The fated day, shall lift her infant hand,
And slaying the usurper, take the throne
Next in the royal line of summer queens.

TO-DAY.

SADDEST prisoner, to death condemned,
Going blindfold, with slow, reluctant feet,
Hands fettered and mute lips, thy doom to meet,
By flaming swords before, behind thee, hemmed,
Led by two Fates, — To-morrow, with her gemmed
Arms that flash mocking tokens of the sweet
Things thou hadst hoped; and Yesterday with cheat
Of withered roses which thou hast contemned,
Decking her icy brow and heavy pall;
While we, mute, helpless, with prophetic black
Have wrapped ourselves, and in thy narrow track
Come, hand in hand, blindfolded, fettered all,
Waiting the hour when, in thy death's last thrall
Bidding us follow thee, thou shalt look back.

OPPORTUNITY.

DO not know if, climbing some steep hill,
   Through fragrant wooded pass, this glimpse
     I bought,
Or whether in some mid-day I was caught
To upper air, where visions of God's will
In pictures to our quickened sense fulfil
His word.   But this I saw.
                  A path I sought
Through wall of rock.   No human fingers wrought
The golden gates which opened sudden, still,
And wide.   My fear was hushed by my delight.
Surpassing fair the lands ; my path lay plain ;
Alas, so spell-bound, feasting on the sight,
I paused, that I but reached the threshold bright,
When, swinging swift, the golden gates again
Were rocky wall, by which I wept in vain.

FLOWERS ON A GRAVE.

I.

WHAT sweeter thing to hear, through tears,
    than this,
Of one who dies, that, looking on him
    dead,
All men with tender reverence gazed and said:
"What courtesy and gentleness were his!
Our ruder lives, for years to come, will miss
His sweet serenity, which daily shed
A grace we scarcely felt, so deep inbred
Of nature was it. Loyalty which is
So loyal as his loyalty to friends
Is rare; such purity is rarer still."
Yes, there is yet one sweeter thing. It ends
The broken speech with sobs that choke and fill
Our throats.
        Alas! lost friend, we knew not how
Our hearts were won to love thee, until now.

II.

SOME lives are bright like torches, and their flame
Casts flickering lights around, and changeful heats;
Some lives blaze like the meteor which fleets
Across the sky; and some of lofty aim

Stand out like beacon-lights.   But never came,
Or can, a light so satisfying sweet,
As steady daylight, unperturbed, complete,
And noiseless.   Human lives we see the same
As this ; their equilibrium so just,
Their movement so serene, so still, small heed
The world pays to their presence till in need
It sudden finds itself. The darkness near,
The precious life returning dust for dust,
It recollects how noon and life were clear.

III.

How poor is all that fame can be or bring !
Although a generation feed the pyre,
How soon dies out the lifeless, loveless fire !
The king is dead.   Hurrah !   Long live the king !
The poet breathes his last.   Who next will sing?
The great man falls.   Who comes to mount still
        higher?
Oh, bitter emptiness of such desire !
Earth holds but one true good, but one true thing,
And this is it — to walk in honest ways
And patient, and with all one's heart belong
In love unto one's own !   No death so strong
That life like this he ever conquers, slays ;
The centuries do to it no hurt, no wrong :
They are eternal resurrection days.

A MEASURE OF HOURS.

UNTO those two I called who hold
In hands omnipotent all lives
Of men, and deal, like gods, such doled
Alms as they list, to him who strives
And him who waits alike:

"Oh! show
Me but how measure ye one hour
Of time, that I at least may know
If I lift up this cross what power
I need; and what I win of bliss
If I may dare to pay the cost —
Whole cost, without which I must miss
This joy, and feel my life lost."
Then Joy spoke first, all breathless:

"Drink!
An hour seems like eternity.
My moments hold whole ages. Think
No price too great which buys for thee
This boundless bliss. Such hours as mine

Mock reckonings. The sands stand still.
Drink quickly! I will give the sign
When it is over. Drink thy fill!"

I had scarce tasted when, with face
All changed and voice grown sharp, Joy cried:
"Thine hour is past. Give place! Give place!
New hearts impatiently abide
Thy going. Every man fills up
His own swift measure. Thou hadst thine.
Who weakly drains the empty cup
Drinks only bitter dregs of wine."

Then Sorrow whispered gently: "Take
This burden up. Be not afraid.
An hour is short. Thou scarce wilt wake
To consciousness that I have laid
My hand upon thee, when the hour
Shall all have passed, and, gladder then
For the brief pain's uplifting power,
Thou shalt but pity griefless men."

I grew by minutes changed and old,
As men change not in many years
Of happiness. Lifetimes untold
Seemed dragging lifeless by. My tears
Ran slow for utter weariness
Of weeping; and, when token came

The hour was done, I felt far less
Of joy than woe; as one whose name
Is called, when prison doors have swung
Open too late, reluctantly
Goes forth to find himself among
Strange faces, desolate, though free.

"O cruel brethren, Joy and Grief,"
I cried, "with equal mockery
Your promises meet our belief.
One blossom and one fruit will be
Your harvest! But full well I know
They are not harvest; only seed
Sown in our tears, from which shall grow
In other soil harvest indeed, —

"Harvest in God's great gardens white,
Where cool and living waters run,
And where the spotless Lamb is light,
Instead of pallid moon and sun;
Where constant through the golden air
The tree of life sheds mystic leaf,
Which angels to the nations bear,
Healing alike their joy and grief."

CHARLOTTE CUSHMAN.

I.

UT yesterday it was. Long years ago
  It seems. The world so altered looks
  to-day
That, journeying idly with my thoughts astray,
I gazed where rose one lofty peak of snow
Above grand tiers on tiers of peaks below.
One moment brief it shone, then sank away,
As swift we reached a point where foot-hills lay
So near they seemed like mountains huge to grow,
And touch the sky. That instant, idly still,
My eye fell on a printed line, and read
Incredulous, with sudden anguished thrill,
The name of this great queen among the dead.
I raised my eyes. The dusty foot-hills near
Had gone. Again the snowy peak shone clear.

II.

OH! thou beloved woman, soul and heart
And life, thou standest unapproached and grand,
As still that glorious snowy peak doth stand.
The dusty barrier our clumsy art

In terror hath called death holds thee apart
From us. 'T is but the low foot-hill of sand
Which bars our vision in a mountain-land.
One moment further on, and we shall start
With speechless joy to find that we have passed
The dusky mound which shuts us from the light
Of thy great love, still quick and warm and fast,
Of thy great strengths, heroically cast,
Of thy great soul, still glowing pure and white,
Of thy great life, still pauseless, full, and bright!

DEDICATION.

I SAW men kneeling where their hands had brought
And fashioned curiously a pile of stone.
To God they said they gave it, for his own,
And that their psalms and prayers had wrought
Its consecration. When, perplexed, I sought
Their meaning, they but answered with a groan,
And called my question blasphemy. Alone,
In silence of the wilderness, I thought
Again. Swift answer came from rock, tree, sod :
" These puny prayers superfluous rise, and late
These psalms. When first the world swung out in
  space,
Amid the shoutings of the sons of God,
Then was its every atom dedicate,
Forever holy by God's gift and grace."

DAWN.

WITH a ring of silver,
    And a ring of gold,
    And a red, red rose
        Which illumines her face,
The sun, like a lover
  Who glows and is bold,
Wooes the lovely earth
    To his strong embrace.

EVE.

IN millions of pieces
    The beautiful rings
    And the scattered petals
        Of the rose so red,
The sun, like a lover
  Who is weary, flings
On the lonely earth
    When the day is dead.

DREAMS.

MYSTERIOUS shapes, with wands of joy and pain,
   Which seize us unaware in helpless sleep,
   And lead us to the houses where we keep
Our secrets hid, well barred by every chain
That we can forge and bind: the crime whose stain
Is slowly fading 'neath the tears we weep;
Dead bliss which, dead, can make our pulses leap —
Oh, cruelty! To make these live again!
They say that death is sleep, and heaven's rest
Ends earth's short day, as, on the last faint gleam
Of sun, our nights shut down, and we are blest.
Let this, then, be of heaven's joy the test,
The proof if heaven be, or only seem,
That we forever choose what we will dream!

THE DAY-STAR IN THE EAST.

I.

EACH morning, in the eastern sky, I see
    The star that morning dares to call its
      own.
    Night's myriads it has outwatched and
      outshone ;
Full radiant dawn pales not its majesty ;
Peer of the sun, his herald fit and free.
Sudden from earth, dark, heavy mists are blown ;
The city's grimy smoke, to pillars grown,
Climbs up the sky, and hides the star from me.
Strange, that a film of smoke can blot a star !
On comes, with blinding glare, the breathless day :
The star is gone. The moon doth surer lay
Than midnight gloom, athwart its light, a bar.
But steadfast as God's angels planets are.
To-morrow's dawn will show its changeless ray.

II.

THE centuries are God's days ; within his hand,
Held in the hollow, as a balance swings,
Less than its dust, are all our temporal things.
Long are his nights, when darkness steeps the land ;

Thousands of years fill one slow dawn's demand;
The human calendar its measure brings,
Feeble and vain, to lift the soul that clings
To hope for light, and seeks to understand.
The centuries are God's days; the greatest least
In his esteem. We have no glass to sweep
His universe. A hand's-breadth distant dies,
To our poor ears, the strain whose echoes keep
All heaven glad. We do but grope and creep.
There always is a day-star in the skies!

OCTOBER'S BRIGHT BLUE WEATHER.

 SUNS and skies and clouds of June,
    And flowers of June together,
Ye cannot rival for one hour
    October's bright blue weather,

When loud the bumble-bee makes haste,
    Belated, thriftless vagrant,
And golden-rod is dying fast,
    And lanes with grapes are fragrant;

When gentians roll their fringes tight
    To save them for the morning,
And chestnuts fall from satin burrs
    Without a sound of warning;

When on the ground red apples lie
    In piles like jewels shining,
And redder still on old stone walls
    Are leaves of woodbine twining;

When all the lovely wayside things
   Their white-winged seeds are sowing,
And in the fields, still green and fair,
   Late aftermaths are growing;

When springs run low, and on the brooks,
   In idle golden freighting,
Bright leaves sink noiseless in the hush
   Of woods, for winter waiting;

When comrades seek sweet country haunts,
   By twos and twos together,
And count like misers hour by hour,
   October's bright blue weather.

O suns and skies and flowers of June,
   Count all your boasts together,
Love loveth best of all the year
   October's bright blue weather.

THE RIVIERA.

PEERLESS shore of peerless sea,
Ere mortal eye had gazed on thee,
What god was lover first of thine,
Drank deep of thy unvintaged wine,
And lying on thy shining breast
Knew all thy passion and thy rest;
And when thy love he must resign,
O generous god, first love of thine,
Left such a dower of wealth to thee,
Thou peerless shore of peerless sea!
Thy balmy air, thy stintless sun,
Thy orange-flowering never done,
Thy myrtle, olive, palm, and pine,
Thy golden figs, thy ruddy wine,
Thy subtle and resistless spell
Which all men feel and none can tell?
O peerless shore of peerless sea!
From all the world we turn to thee;
No wonder deem we thee divine!
Some god was lover first of thine.

SEMITONES.

AH me, the subtle boundary between
    What pleases and what pains! The dif-
        ference
Between the word that thrills our every sense
With joy and one which hurts, although it mean
No hurt! It is the things that are unseen,
Invisible, not things of violence,
For which the mightiest are without defence.
On kine most fair to see one may grow lean
With hunger. Many a snowy bread is doled
Which is far harder than the hardest stones.
'T is but a narrow line divides the zones
Where suns are warm from those where suns are
    cold.
'Twixt harmonies divine as chords can hold
And torturing discords, lie but semitones!

IN THE DARK.

AS one who journeys on a stormy night
    Through mountain passes which he does
      not know
Shields like his life from savage gusts that blow
The swaying flame of his frail torch's light,
So each of us through life's long groping fight
Clings fast to one dear faith, one love, whose glow
Makes darkness noonday to our trusting sight,
And joys of perils into which we go.
God help us, when this precious shining mark
The raging storms of deep distrust assail
With icy, poisoned breath and deadly aim,
Till we, with hearts that shrink and cower and quail
In terror which no measure has nor name,
Stand trembling, helpless, palsied, in the dark.

MORDECAI.

MAKE friends with him! He is of royal line,
    Although he sits in rags. Not all of thine
Array of splendor, pomp of high estate,
Can buy him from his place within the gate,
The King's Gate of thy happiness, where he,
Yes, even he, the Jew, remaineth free,
Never obeisance making, never scorn
Betraying of thy silver and new-born
Delight. Make friends with him, for unawares
The charmèd secret of thy joys he bears;
Be glad, so long as his black sackcloth, late
And early, thwarts thy sun; for if in hate
And haste thou plottest for his blood, thy own death-cry,
Not his, comes from the gallows fifty cubits high.

IN APRIL.

WHAT did the sparrow do yesterday?
    Nobody knew but the sparrows;
    He were too bold who should try to say;
They have forgotten it all to-day.
Why does it haunt my thoughts this way,
  With a joy that piques and harrows,
    As the birds fly past,
    And the chimes ring fast,
And the long spring shadows sweet shadow cast?

There's a maple-bud redder to-day;
  It will almost flower to-morrow;
I could swear 't was only yesterday
In a sheath of snow and ice it lay,
With fierce winds blowing it every way;
  Whose surety had it to borrow,
    Till birds should fly past,
    And chimes ring fast,
And the long spring shadows sweet shadow cast?

IN APRIL.

"Was there ever a day like to-day,
  So clear, so shining, so tender?"
The old cry out; and the children say,
With a laugh, aside: "That's always the way
With the old, in spring; as long as they stay,
  They find in it greater splendor,
    When the birds fly past,
    And the chimes ring fast,
And the long spring shadows sweet shadow cast!"

Then that may be why my thoughts all day —
  I see I am old, by the token —
Are so haunted by sounds, now sad, now gay,
Of the words I hear the sparrows say,
And the maple-bud's mysterious way
  By which from its sheath it has broken,
    While the birds fly past,
    And the chimes ring fast,
And the long spring shadows sweet shadow cast!

TWO HARVESTS.

I.

BLOSSOM and fruit no man could count or hoard;
Seasons their laws forgot, in riot haste
Lavishing yield on yield in madman's waste;
No tropic with its centuries' heat outpoured
In centuries of summers, ever stored
Such harvest. Had the earth her sole pearl placed
In wine of sun to melt, — one blissful taste
To drain and die, — it had not fully dowered
This harvest! She who smiling goes, a queen,
Reaping with alabaster arms and hands
The fruits and flowers of these magic lands,
With idle, satiate intervals between, —
Oh, what to her do laws of harvest mean?
Joy passes by her, where she laden stands!

II.

A PARCHED and arid land, all colorless,
Than desert drearier, than rock more stern;
Spring could not find, nor any summer learn
The secret to redeem this wilderness.
Harsh winds sweep through with icy storm and stress:
Fierce lurid suns shine but to blight and burn;
And streams rise, pallid, but to flee and turn:
Who soweth here waits miracle to bless
The harvest! She who smiling goes, a queen,
Seeking with hidden tears and tireless hands
To win a fruitage from these barren lands, —
She knoweth what the laws of harvest mean!
Blades spring, flowers bloom, by all but her unseen;
Joy's halo crowns her, where she patient stands!

HABEAS CORPUS.

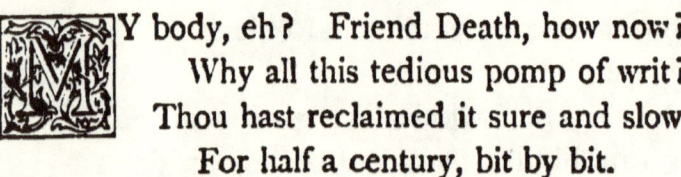Y body, eh? Friend Death, how now?
   Why all this tedious pomp of writ?
Thou hast reclaimed it sure and slow
   For half a century, bit by bit.

In faith thou knowest more to-day
   Than I do, where it can be found!
This shrivelled lump of suffering clay,
   To which I now am chained and bound,

Has not of kith or kin a trace
   To the good body once I bore;
Look at this shrunken, ghastly face:
   Didst ever see that face before?

Ah, well, friend Death, good friend thou art;
   Thy only fault thy lagging gait,
Mistaken pity in thy heart
   For timorous ones that bid thee wait.

Do quickly all thou hast to do,
   Nor I nor mine will hindrance make ;
I shall be free when thou art through ;
   I grudge thee nought that thou must take !

Stay ! I have lied ; I grudge thee one,
   Yes, two I grudge thee at this last, —
Two members which have faithful done
   My will and bidding in the past.

I grudge thee this right hand of mine ;
   I grudge thee this quick-beating heart ;
They never gave me coward sign,
   Nor played me once a traitor's part.

I see now why in olden days
   Men in barbaric love or hate
Nailed enemies' hands at wild crossways,
   Shrined leaders' hearts in costly state :

The symbol, sign, and instrument
   Of each soul's purpose, passion, strife,
Of fires in which are poured and spent
   Their all of love, their all of life.

O feeble, mighty human hand !
   O fragile, dauntless human heart !
The universe holds nothing planned
   With such sublime, transcendent art !

HABEAS CORPUS.

Yes, Death, I own I grudge thee mine
  Poor little hand, so feeble now;
Its wrinkled palm, its altered line,
  Its veins so pallid and so slow —

  . . . (Unfinished here.)

Ah, well, friend Death, good friend thou art;
  I shall be free when thou art through.
Take all there is — take hand and heart;
  There must be somewhere work to do.

A LAST PRAYER.

FATHER, I scarcely dare to pray,
   So clear I see, now it is done,
That I have wasted half my day,
   And left my work but just begun;

So clear I see that things I thought
   Were right or harmless were a sin;
So clear I see that I have sought,
   Unconscious, selfish aims to win;

So clear I see that I have hurt
   The souls I might have helped to save;
That I have slothful been, inert,
   Deaf to the calls thy leaders gave.

In outskirts of thy kingdoms vast,
   Father, the humblest spot give me;
Set me the lowliest task thou hast;
   Let me repentant work for thee!

THE SONG HE NEVER WROTE.

HIS thoughts were song, his life was singing;
    Men's hearts like harps he held and smote,
But in his heart went ever ringing,
    Ringing, the song he never wrote.

Hovering, pausing, luring, fleeting,
    A farther blue, a brighter mote,
The vanished sound of swift winds meeting,
    The opal swept beneath the boat.

A gleam of wings forever flaming,
    Never folded in nest or cote;
Secrets of joy, past name or naming;
    Measures of bliss past dole or rote;

Echoes of music, always flying,
    Always echo, never the note;
Pulses of life, past life, past dying,—
    All these in the song he never wrote.

THE SONG HE NEVER WROTE.

Dead at last, and the people, weeping,
    Turned from his grave with wringing hands, —
"What shall we do, now he lies sleeping,
    His sweet song silent in our lands?

"Just as his voice grew clearer, stronger," —
    This was the thought that keenest smote, —
"O Death! couldst thou not spare him longer?
    Alas for the songs he never wrote!"

Free at last, and his soul up-soaring,
    Planets and skies beneath his feet,
Wonder and rapture all out-pouring,
    Eternity how simple, sweet!

Sorrow slain, and every regretting,
    Love and Love's labors left the same,
Weariness over, suns without setting,
    Motion like thought on wings of flame:

Higher the singer rose and higher,
    Heavens, in spaces, sank like bars;
Great joy within him glowed like fire,
    He tossed his arms among the stars, —

"This is the life, past life, past dying;
  I am I, and I live the life:
Shame on the thought of mortal crying!
  Shame on its petty toil and strife!

"Why did I halt, and weakly tremble?"
  Even in heaven the memory smote,—
"Fool to be dumb, and to dissemble!
  Alas for the song I never wrote!"

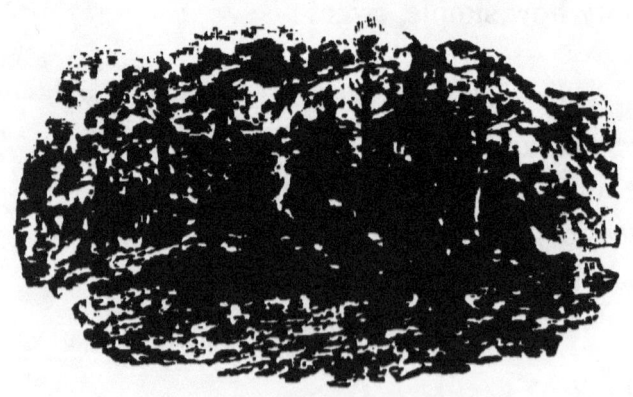

www.ingramcontent.com/pod-product-compliance
Lightning Source LLC
Chambersburg PA
CBHW030732230426
43667CB00007B/688